Limited edition

Prototypes, One-Offs and Design Art Furniture

Sophie Lovell

Birkhäuser
Basel · Boston · Berlin

Aylin Kayser and Christian Metzner • Ikarus
Wax lampshades that melt into new
forms from the heat of their light bulbs
© Christian Metzner

For the wheel's still in spin

And there's no tellin' who
That it's namin'.

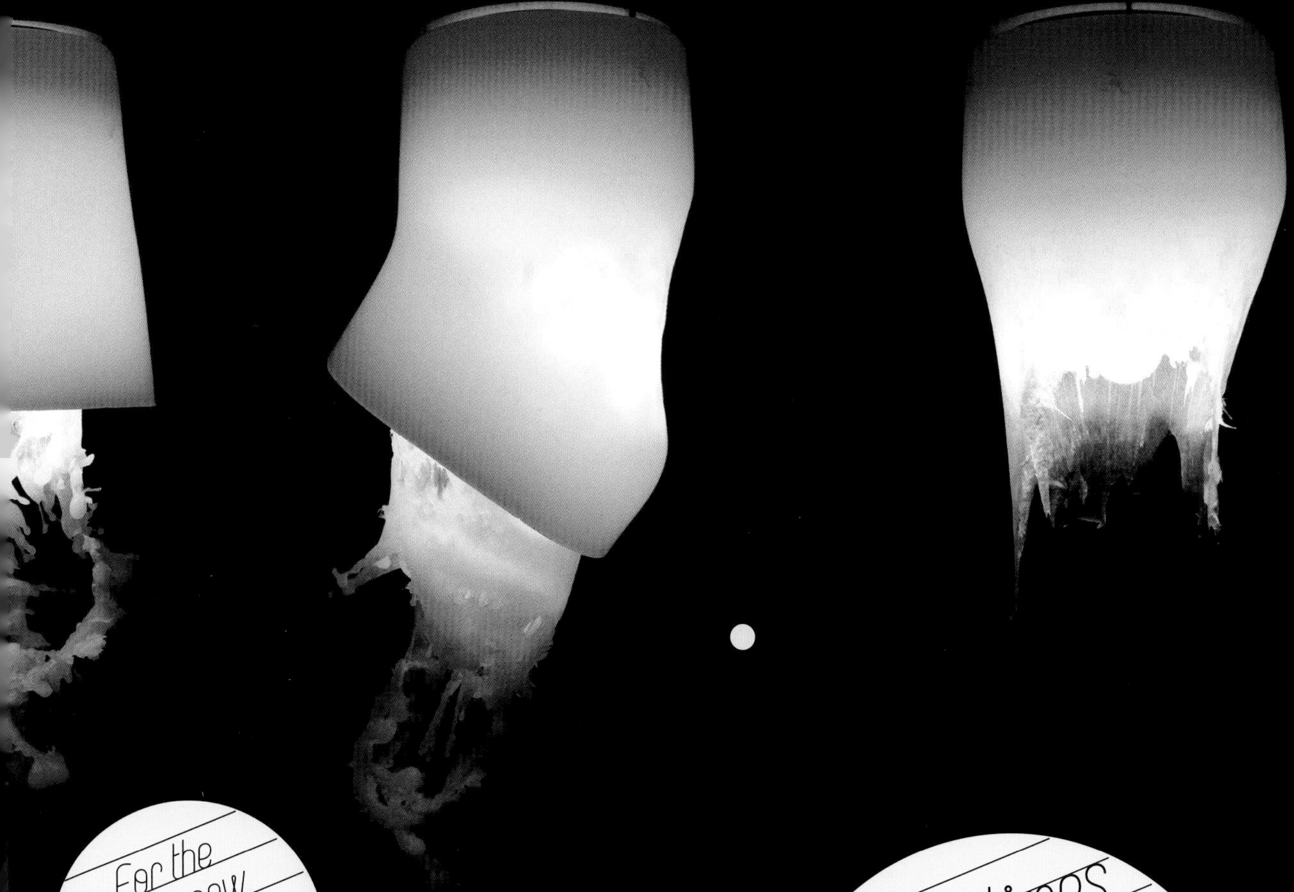

For the loser now
Will be later to win

For the times they are a-changin'.

Bob Dylan

introduction

Our modern world is hard to pin down. It is filled with complexity and an ever-expanding wealth of interconnecting layers. We are experiencing an era of flux defined by change, hybridisation and exploration. The fruits of centuries of experience are being remixed with innovation and digitalisation. These are exciting yet confusing times. The realm of design, like many other disciplines, is now challenged to fulfil an increasing number of roles: to keep up with new materials and technologies; to facilitate interfaces with our increasing technological dependence; to help make the world a better and more sustainable place, yet balance that somehow with the demand for the trophies of conspicuous consumption and an unquenchable desire for novelty. Added to this burden of responsibility is the fact that the discipline itself has become a huge field with no clearly defined boundaries.

Design is traditionally about working to find solutions and achieve goals within a set of limitations or restrictions usually dictated by materials, manufacturing techniques, price, function and aesthetics. But today many designers do not simply deliver products, they design processes, interfaces and systems, working in two, three and even four dimensions. While for some the workplace may be almost entirely in the virtual realm of calculations and CAD programmes, others are to be found in their workshops, ankle-deep in wood shavings, forming and shaping objects by hand – much as other craftspeople have done for thousands of years before them. Still other designers make objects that appear to have no function at all, or intentionally create self-referring sketches of ideas that seem to solve nothing and go nowhere.

Limited Edition is about designers who make furniture objects outside of the industrial manufacturing system. Although some employ the same criteria, tools and materials as those required to produce many hundreds or thousands of copies of an object, this book is about individuals working on the peripheries of that system, and the work of those who have chosen to step outside it completely. Many of the designers in this book think of themselves as explorers, testing the boundaries of materials, process and medium. For them, the product almost seems to be an afterthought or added extra. These designers are committed to experimentation; to exploring not just the nature and forms of what they produce but also the systems within which they are commissioned, created, received, displayed, appraised and used. There is also a growing band of gallerists, patrons and curators who are nurturing and encouraging these experiments in the form of one-offs, prototypes or limited editions. They are helping to create new connections between design and the market, between product and object, between industry and ideas: changing attitudes and challenging structures.

Tord Boontje • The Fig Leaf
Hand-painted enamelled copper leaves, lost wax cast patinated bronze tree, hand-dyed and woven silk, hand-formed tracery support structure, trompe l'oeil back
Client: Meta
© Marcus Gaab

Pablo Reinoso • Spaghetti Bâle
Gallery: Carpenters Workshop Gallery
© Pablo Reinoso Studio

Pablo Reinoso • Spaghetti Ballade bench
© Pablo Reinoso Studio

Either consciously or unconsciously, these individuals are asking some big questions. What is design? What does it mean to call oneself a designer? What are the roles of objects and products? If design is to provide so many solutions, where does it have to go to find new answers, to extend beyond itself and the boundaries of its own limitations? Which constraints are now negotiable for design as a discipline, and which are non-negotiable? It is hard to find answers – especially when the very issues involved are in such a nascent stage of change that we have not even developed an appropriate vocabulary with which to discuss them. Many of the designers I spoke to whilst writing this book found it hard to put names or categories to what they were doing and how they were working. We need the perspective of time and the luxury of a hindsight that we do not yet have. What we can do, however, is look at patterns and choose examples and individuals who seem to be looking at, evaluating and producing objects in a different way.

Limited Edition is a highly selective opinion poll on the state of furniture design at the borders of industry and outside of it. In over forty interviews with designers, manufacturers, gallerists, auctioneers and critics, I have attempted to sift and arrange some of their thoughts and comments into broad groups and areas that seem to represent some patterns or parallels. It may be old-fashioned to do so, but I have also tried to break down this new world of explorative design objects into categories. It is not a taxonomy by any means – the styles, forms and materials are far too diverse for that – but rather a loose categorisation according to intent on the part of the designer, curator or patron, as well as the ways in which they are collaborating with one another. Categories – however loose they may be – do tend to aid discussion and communication. Nevertheless, this book is by no means comprehensive. I would be the first to admit that this survey is limited in its scope and there are other voices that also deserve to be heard. My aim has been to give a brief insight into the dazzling creative array of work out there and, I hope, to encourage further discourse rather than jump to premature or dogmatic conclusions. If I have succeeded, Limited Edition is not just a book about beautiful things, but hopefully provides food for thought as well.

You could consider design in general to be a luxury. But if design is good I prefer to call it cultural and that's not luxurious, that's adding to the quality of its life, regardless of its price.

Richard Hutten

8

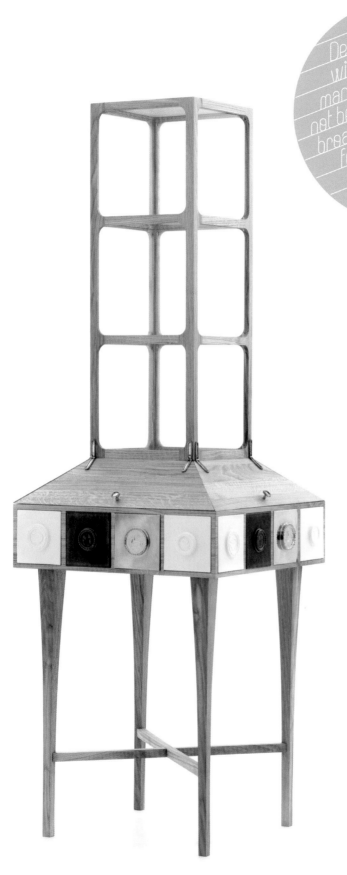

Design today, with its myriad manifestations, does not bear the same kind of broad, unified theoretical foundation that some believe once underpinned Modernism.

Instead the field is characterised by a rich heterogeneity of ideas. Limited-edition work is only one of these manifestations, but is one of the most exciting because it includes some of the most beautiful, poetic and progressive objects being created at this time.

Wava Carpenter

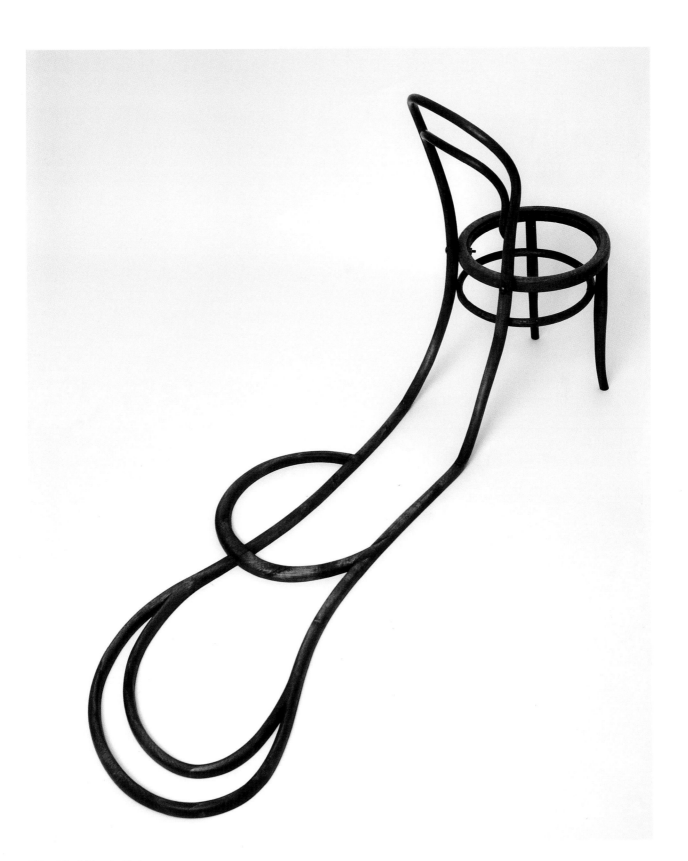

Kiki van Eijk • Patchwork cabinet
© Frank Tielemans

Pablo Reinoso • TH 14 05 Chaise
© Carlos Yebra

Yael Mer & Shay Alkalay – Raw-Edges Design Studio • Stack
Clients: Gradual, Johnson Trading Gallery and a production
version for Established & Sons
© Shay Alkalay

Yael Mer & Shay Alkalay – Raw-Edges Design Studio • Stack
Client: Established & Sons
© Mike Golderwater

Design is a young discipline. It has many aspects and is still developing.
Ralf Fehlbaum

Tokujin Yoshioka • Water block
Edition of 8+2+8
Gallery: Design Miami/Basel, December 2007
© Nacása & Partners Inc.

Tokujin Yoshioka • Rainbow chair
Edition of 8
Gallery: Design Miami/Basel, December 2007
© Nacása & Partners Inc.

Joris Laarman • Bone armchair
A computer-generated 'natural' form; edition of 12
© Jacob Krupnick

Markus Benesch Creates • Architect's Hatch
Series of 13, each limited to an edition of 6 pieces
Gallery: Galerie Maurer
© Patrick Spaeth, Benni Konte

I'm trying to push the boundaries of my profession and my profession is making functional pieces for a market.

Hella Jongerius

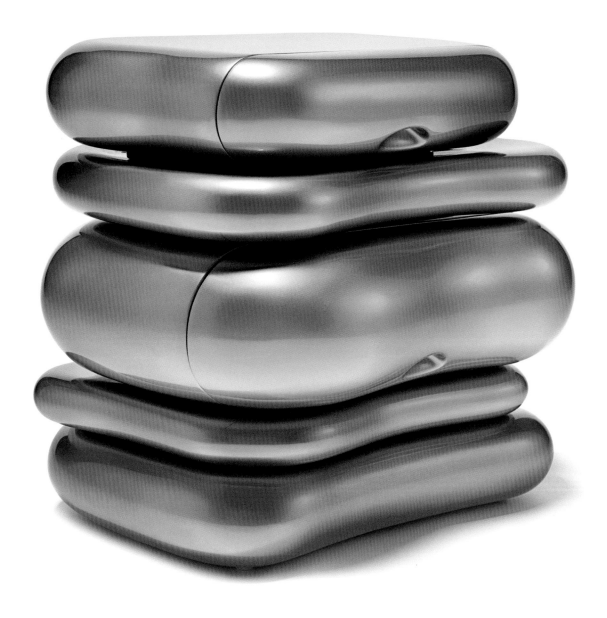

Some people can't have the 'sick' luxury of being 'sick' of mass production', of mass production', for most people, that is all they can afford.

And that is why limited-edition experimentation, what Sottsass called 'theoretical design', is so important – it is often the originator/embryo of what may end up on the mass market, hopefully making people's lives better.

Johanna Grawunder

Mattia Bonetti • Heather chest of drawers
Edition of 8, 2 artist's proofs and 2 prototypes
Gallery: David Gill Galleries
© David Gill Galleries
Photo: Thomas Brown

Mattia Bonetti • Toast chest of drawers
Edition of 8, 2 artist's proofs and 2 prototypes
Gallery: David Gill Galleries
© David Gill Galleries
Photo: Thomas Brown

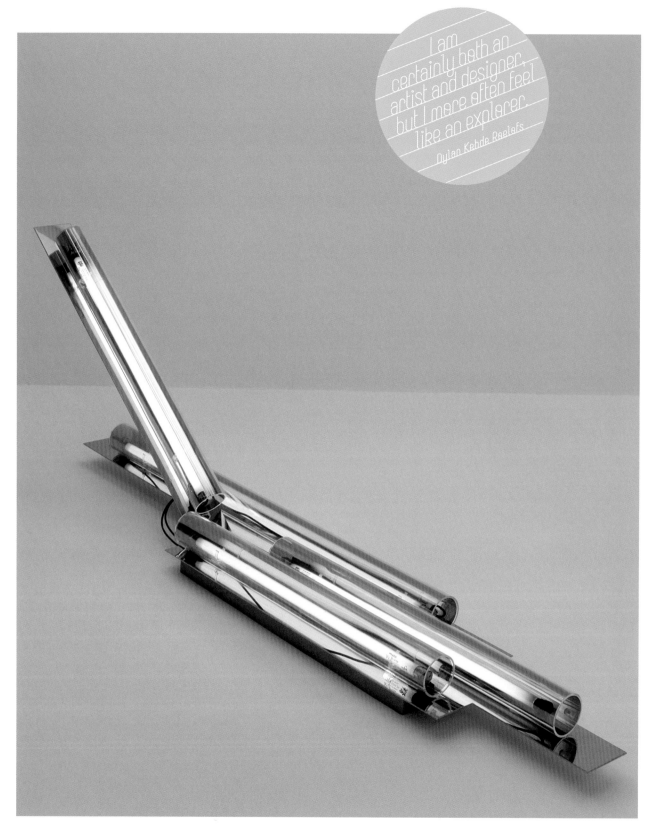

I am
certainly both an
artist and designer,
but I more often feel
like an explorer.
Dylan Kehde Roelofs

Olivier Peyricot • 16 Hz programmable lamp
One-off
Gallery: ToolsGalerie
© Marc Domage

Mathieu Lehanneur • Irrésistibles Reflets
Client: Christofle, Paris
© Cyril Afsa

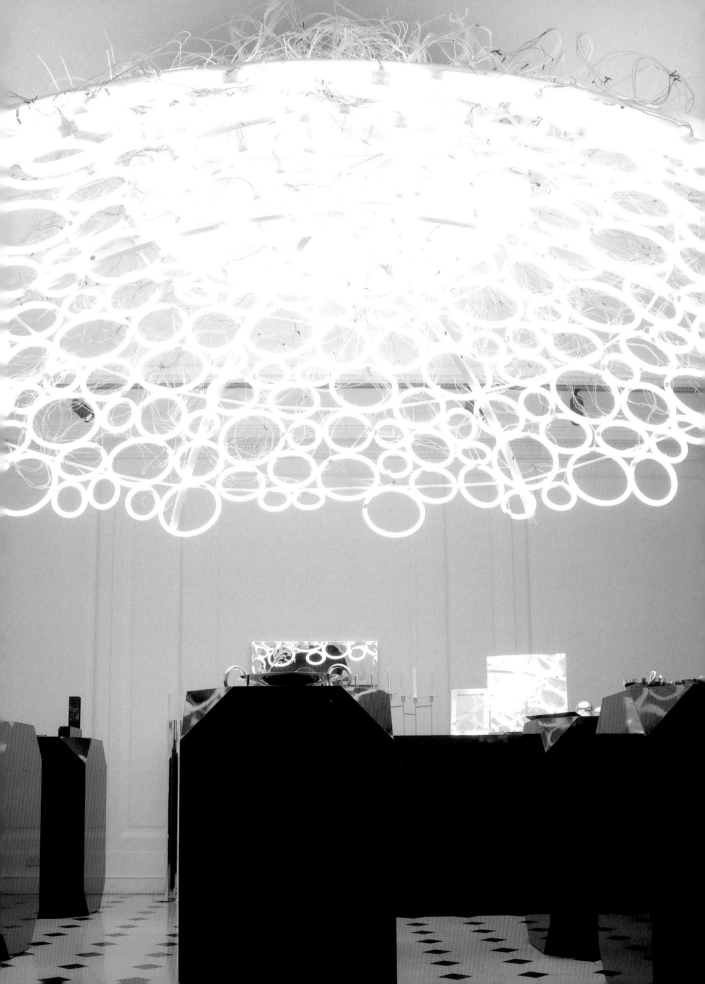

Markus Benesch Creates • Bavarian Flair
Series of 4, each limited to an edition of 3
© Patrick Spaeth, Benni Konte

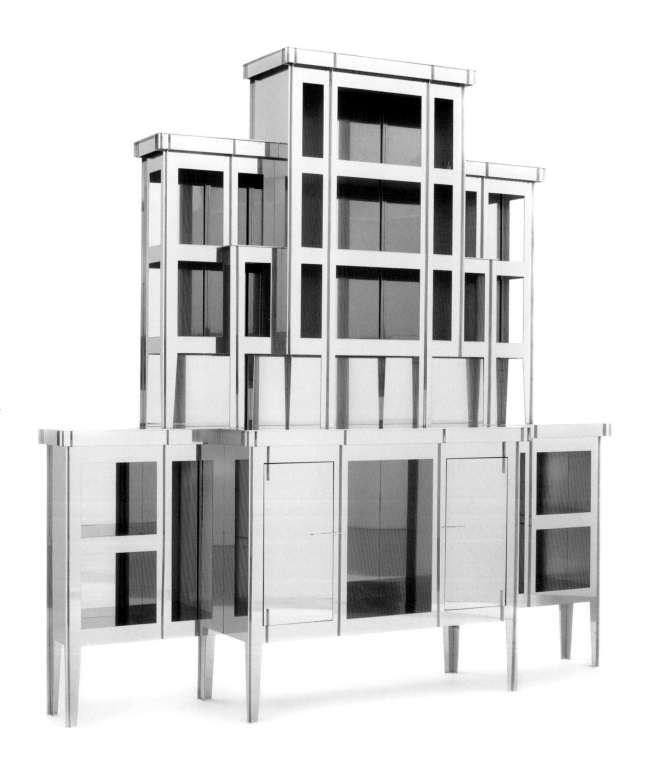

We will look back on NOW and call it some term. And that will provide titles for all of the people working at solitary pieces within such a mass production atmosphere and all of the people that cross disciplines.

Gerd Peteran

Joost van Bleiswijk • Big-heavy-cabinet
Edition of 8 and 2 artist's proofs
© Frank Tielemans

Joost van Bleiswijk • Little Clock
© Frank Tielemans

Joost van Bleiswijk • No Screw No Glue
Edition of 8 and 2 artist's proofs
© Frank Tielemans

The job
of designers is
to improve things. If
awareness of good design
is more widespread, that
can only lead to overall
better quality of consumer
products – for us all.
Marc Newson

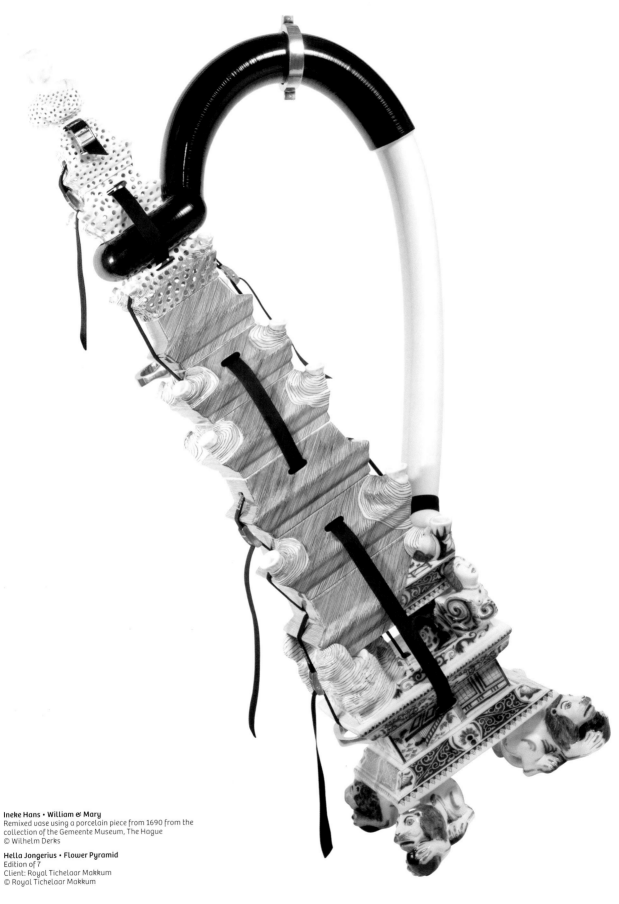

Ineke Hans · William & Mary
Remixed vase using a porcelain piece from 1690 from the
collection of the Gemeente Museum, The Hague
© Wilhelm Derks

Hella Jongerius · Flower Pyramid
Edition of 7
Client: Royal Tichelaar Makkum
© Royal Tichelaar Makkum

Gerold Tusch • Frames IV
One-off
© Gerold Tusch

Kiki van Eijk • Soft dressing table
Textiles and ceramics
© Frank Tielemans

There may well be objects that spring fully formed from the heads of their creators, but as a rule the design process is a long and painstaking path filled with sketches, models, materials studies and technical trials. When a design leaves the page, or the computer screen, and becomes solid and three-dimensional, it enters the realm of the prototype.

As its name suggests, the prototype is the first of its kind: a little rough and imperfect perhaps, but the first clear example of its type nonetheless. The implication is that there will be more to follow. The prototype is traditionally the phase or moment between concept and series for industrial designers. It is what Augustin Scott de Martinville from Big-game calls 'the materialisation of an idea'. Everything else that follows can be called refinement or compromise – depending on how you want to look at it. Although the moment in which a successful prototype is completed can be an extremely exciting one for the designer, it really is just a stage in the design process, as the model is either improved upon or cast aside.

Although prototypes tend to be handmade or individually machined, and focused towards testing structure, form or materials rather than achieving perfection, they are sometimes finished to such a high degree that they could pass for completed objects in their own right. From a collector's point of view, this makes certain prototypes of well-known and rather common objects both valuable and highly desirable. We are all familiar with the first tubular steel Wassily chair from 1925 by Marcel Breuer or the first ever solid plastic cantilevered chair from 1960 by Verner Panton. They were both highly innovative, not to say revolutionary, designs of their day, and both went into successful mass production. You can buy a new Panton stackable chair now for around 200 euros, and the Wassily is still widely available from a number of manufacturers. But what if the first ever prototype of the cantilevered chair – or Breuer's first workshop attempt – were to come into your possession? They would represent moments at which their designers first breathed life into ideas that were to become major milestones in twentieth-century design. They would be utterly unique, and if the market for such objects were hot – which it is these days – then they would be (and are) worth a fortune. Buying a designer's prototype is about originality, not perfection, says London-based designer Rolf Sachs. 'For the collector it is very special because it has something that he knows is the mother of a future thing.'

Big-game • Metal Work
Aluminium prototype
© ECAL
Photo: Florian Joye

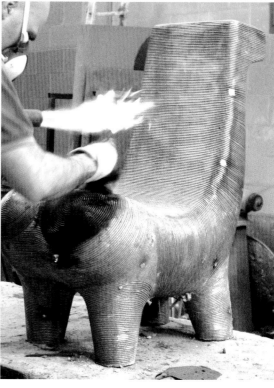

The high-end collectors' market has come to view prototypes of series furniture as investment opportunities. They enjoy a status on a par with handmade or one-off pieces. Whereas this phenomenon began in the vintage section of twentieth-century design as a way of collecting special pieces that were part of a series or mass production era, the tendency has now spread to contemporary prototypes from established or even young designers. There is some confusion, however, as to the meaning of the term 'prototype' in this respect. On the one hand, there are product or furniture designers who still work very much within the industrial system and their prototypes fulfil the traditional role of testing and communicating changes within the design process of a product. Yet others create prototypes that are closer to sketches, maquettes or pieces of sculpture that have far more to do with the creative concept than any form of product. And there are some designers who do both: Amsterdam-based Satyendra Pakhalé, for example, designs pieces for series production for the likes of Magis, Cor Unum and Cappellini, but he also conducts his own experiments with materials and processes that can result in works – like his B.M. Horse Chair and Ceramic Chairs – that then find their way onto the gallery market. These are what he calls 'studio projects', and they can involve many years of research. His Horse Chair took some seven years to perfect, and involved numerous scale models and 3D CAD designs. But, he says, it is only the first piece made to scale in the 'real material – like the bronze lost wax casting process in the case of the Horse Chair', that he is prepared to call a 'prototype'.

German designer Konstantin Grcic also considers himself first and foremost an industrial designer. He often works with extremely high-tech materials and processes to engineer new forms intended to end up as good, functional, affordable products in the tradition of twentieth-century German industrial design that arose from Bauhaus, Ulm and the Deutsche Werkbund. Once again, prototypes in this sense are simply an essential part of the development process toward mass production. As Pierre Keller, director of the Swiss design college ECAL, puts it: 'A prototype is a step in the design process. It can stop there, but if it does it means that it has failed. In order to be successful, a prototype has to be followed by industrial development or multiple editions.' In the context of this system, Keller is right, but Grcic is well aware that design is changing – and with it, the role of the prototype. The ways in which he has documented and displayed his products in recent years indicate a preoccupation with process and experimentation that puts the prototype on a pedestal – rather than the product.

We don't have
a great relationship
any more with what we
buy. People are looking into
ways of giving new value to
the products they buy and to
create a relationship with
them. One of the ways is to
be aware of the way it
is made.

Sarah van Gameren

For the collector the prototype is very special because it has something that he knows is the mother of a future thing.
Rolf Sachs

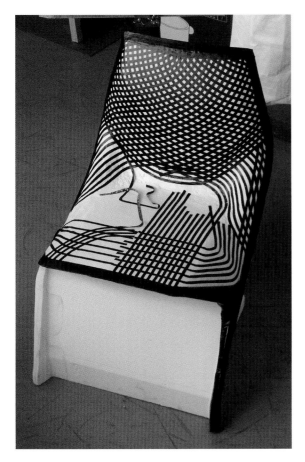

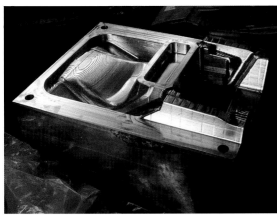

Studio Hausen • Crooner lamps
Prototypes
© Studio Hausen
Photo: Daniel Schulze

Konstantin Grcic • MYTO chair
Development models and mould
Client: BASF / Plank
© Konstantin Grcic Industrial Design

Konstantin Grcic • Stacked MYTO chairs
Client: BASF / Plank
© Konstantin Grcic Industrial Design

A pertinent example here would be Grcic's new MYTO chair for Plank, which is the first single block, all-plastic cantilevered chair on the market since Panton's 1960 creation. The chair is an impressive piece of design engineering made possible thanks to a new plastic developed by the chemical giant BASF and intense collaboration between designer, materials manufacturer, producer, toolmaker and machine builders. When it was launched with its own show, parallel to the 2008 Salone del Mobile in Milan, the emphasis was not so much on the final product as on the prototypes and the processes involved in its development. Rows of different prototypes marking the path of the chair's creation were displayed in an industrial-looking environment situated in a gallery space. The whole thing was staged so precisely that it bordered on an art installation. The prototypes in this instance were the focal point of the installation and celebrated as beautiful objects in their own right, even though they were not usable as chairs.

À propos 'art', there is an increasing number of autarkic designer-producers or 'creators' who have studios and workshops where they both design and produce their own work in small quantities. They have not completely divorced themselves from the democratic design system, whose primary goal is to design many products for everyone, but rather appear to be practising an update of the pre-industrial mindset that does not separate the fine arts from the applied arts. Rolf Sachs: 'If somebody is a créateur, they can be an artist or a furniture designer because everything they do has a creative aspect… I feel closer to the soul of an artist than a designer, because I try to develop new ideas which somebody else might pick up on later and turn into mass production pieces.' This new generation of designer-producers is highly conscious of the prototype's dual role as both a desirable object and an industrial template. Augustin Scott de Martinville says: 'When we work for galleries such as Kreo in Paris, we make objects that are "prototypes". Sometimes we use what we've learned from that to make industrial products. The Wood Work lamp for Kreo followed by the Metal Work edition (see page 30) is a good example. The original Wood Work was a really daring object made of super-light balsa wood. It had to be handcrafted. The industrial version uses the visual language we developed from the first version, and the same principles, but is adapted to large-scale production.'

The young Berlin designer duo Studio Hausen take this commercial role of the prototype a step further and use it to court new clients: 'The prototype is the core element of our work. It is a statement. We believe that designers are idea generators. Our products are ideas in the shape of prototypes. In order to get noticed we need to communicate our ideas at trade fairs, exhibitions and in the media. This requires a constant output, because only those with the best ideas get documented in the competition for attention.' For Studio Hausen, the prototype is expression and marketing tool in one, although its original function remains the same, namely: 'the model upon which a later analogue series can be based.'

Prototypes in this role become a means by which the rather slower process of industrial product development can keep pace with a world hungry for novelty and innovation. They are a vehicle for acquiring media presence through which smaller independent designers gain critical and industry attention. This may be followed by contracts with manufacturers or commissions by galleries to develop the idea further – be it as mass product or limited-edition series. Both options will bring financial input with which the designers can finance their next round of ideas. There are distinct similarities here with the fashion industry, where fashion designers produce new collections – essentially prototypes worn by models – at specific seasonal events each year.

Sarah van Gameren • Big Dipper
Mechanical performance installation making wax chandeliers
© Sarah van Gameren

Going back to Grcic's tactic of exhibiting both prototypes and process to launch a product: the prototypes here also provide a narrative element that helps market the MYTO chair. This technique is becoming increasingly prevalent amongst designers; other notable examples include Ronan and Erwan Bouroullec, Stefan Diez and Pieke Bergmans. This form of display gives the chair a story, a history, and strongly connects the names of the designer-producer and material manufacturer to the product along the way. In today's multimedia environment we are surrounded by so many visual stimuli and 'things' to buy, that increasingly refined strategies are required to fend off a growing level of consumer fatigue. 'We don't have a great relationship any more with what we buy,' says Dutch designer Sarah van Gameren. 'People are looking into ways of giving new value to the products they buy and to create a relationship with them. One of the ways is to be aware of the way it is made.' As part of the London-based partnership Studio Glithero, van Gameren's products and prototypes are created on-site in galleries and exhibition spaces. She introduces a temporal aspect to her designs by using the design process as spectacle to display what she calls her 'experiments'. With her Big Dipper (see page 36), for example, van Gameren exhibits a large machine that dips intricately shaped wick constructions into wax to create candles shaped like candelabras, in what is essentially a kinetic performance. The resulting objects are not strictly prototypes but they are rough, slightly unfinished-looking and – despite being machine-made – essentially unique. 'That's where prototype and experimentation come really close,' explains van Gameren. 'With the Big Dipper there is a double spotlight: one on the end product and one on the process. Without the timeline they can't exist.'

Rolf Sachs welcomes this new narrative element in design. 'It is exactly what people want and exactly what I'm trying to do... to bring depth to the object, a sense of community perhaps, a sense of history, away from the clean, just purely functional, object.' He even adds: 'We have to go much further; we're not courageous enough at the moment.'

Adding narrative to the design process is not only about ennui and hard marketing ploys. By understanding where something comes from and how it is made, consumers are empowered to take responsibility for their consumption. If you are unhappy with the story, you can choose not to buy the product. On the other hand, if you like the story you may choose to buy the product because of it. The purchasing decision no longer has to be made on aesthetic criteria alone. 'This gives the product sophistication,' says Scott de Martinville. 'It's a bit like organic food: you are ready to accept flaws because you know where the product comes from. You even like it more because of these flaws.'

El Ultimo Grito • Hump
Prototypes & Experiments exhibition, 2007
Client: La Casa Encendida, Madrid
Gallery: The Aram Gallery
© Shira Klasmer

Gitta Gschwendtner • Shuttlecock Chandelier
Prototypes & Experiments exhibition, 2007
Gallery: The Aram Gallery
© Shira Klasmer

Studio Makkink & Bey • S.L.A.K.
Prototypes & Experiments exhibition, 2007
Gallery: The Aram Gallery
© Shira Klasmer

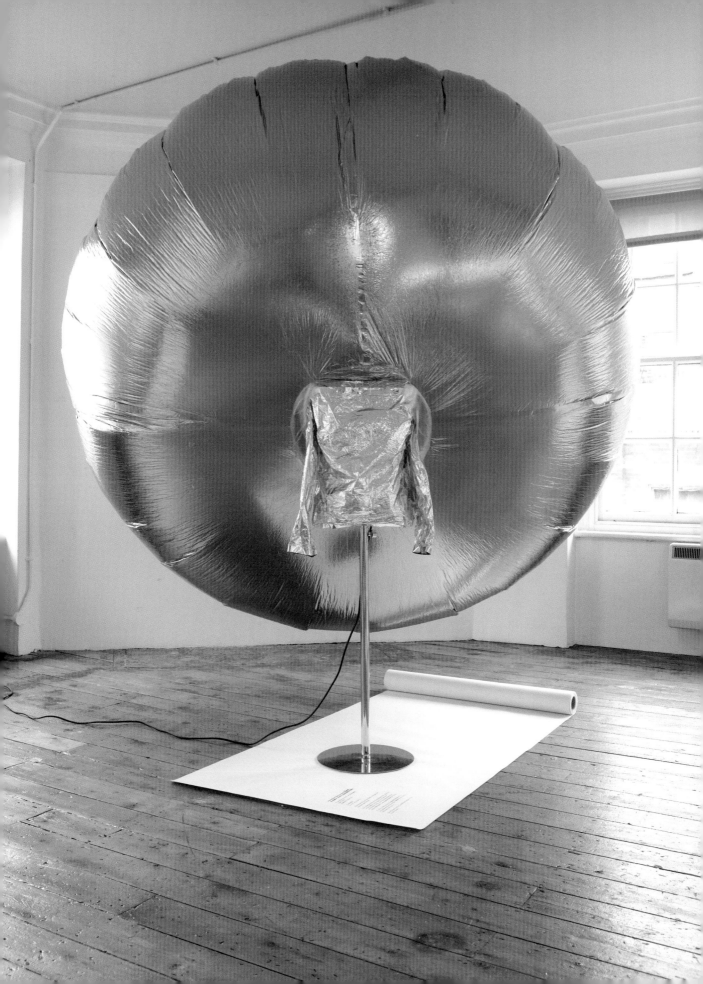

Sarah van Gameren • Burn Burn Burn
One-off performance using flammable paint
© Sarah van Gameren

Hella Jongerius • Props
Prototypes
© Bob Goedewaagen

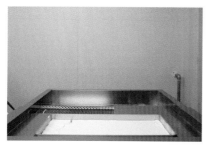

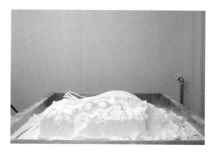

Nendo • Diamond chair (in production)
Chair structure based on the atomic configuration of
a diamond. Produced using powder sintering rapid
prototyping, where a laser guided by 3D CAD data
transforms polyamide particles into a hard framework
© Masayuki Hayashi

Nendo • Diamond chair
Rapid prototype
© Masayuki Hayashi

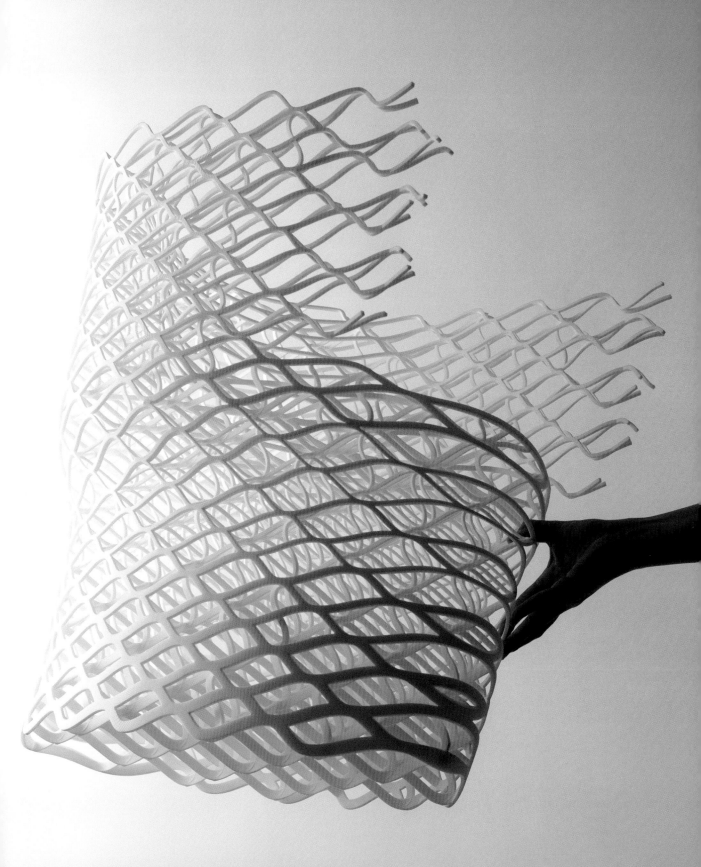

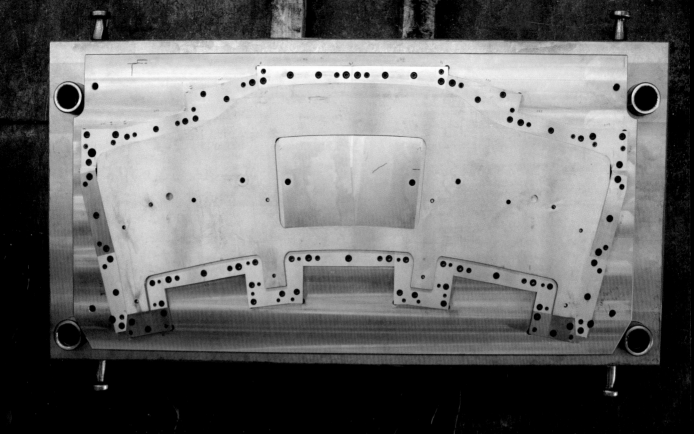

Ronan and Erwan Bouroullec • Steelwood chair (in production)
Client: Magis, Italy
© Studio Bouroullec

Ronan and Erwan Bouroullec · Slow chair
Prototype
Client: Vitra, Switzerland
© Paul Tahon & Ronan and Erwan Bouroullec

Eva Marguerre · Nido stool and table series
Prototypes
© Ulrike Myrzik

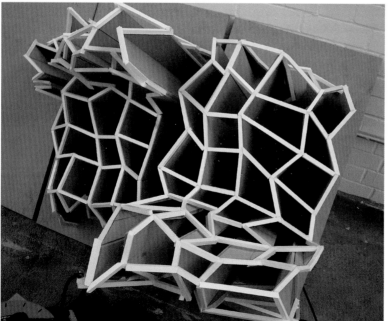

Eric Degenhardt • Cup armchair
Cardboard prototype
Client: Richard Lampert
Prototypes photo shoot for Park Avenue magazine, Germany, 2007
© Photo: Marcus Gaab

Julian Mayor • Burnout model
Client: TENT
© Julian Mayor

**Jakob Gebert + Neuland Industriedesign • Tischmich folding table
+ Insert Coin shelving system**
Prototypes
Client: Nils Holger Moormann
Prototypes photo shoot for Park Avenue magazine, Germany, 2007
© Photo: Marcus Gaab

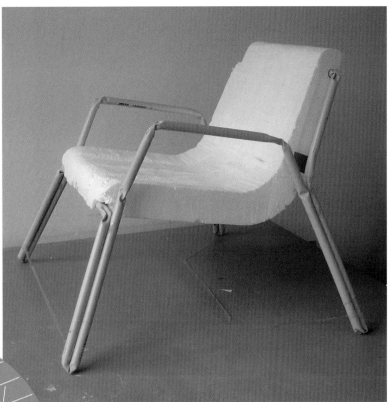

Process is amazing. Showing it is great. It's a general trend. Today we have TV shows on the making of pop bands, so why not design? The risk is that we'll get the same type of design as pop bands – artificial.

Augustin Scott de Martinville

Werner Aisslinger • Rol chair seat
Prototype
Client: Viccarbe
Prototypes photo shoot for Park Avenue magazine, Germany, 2007
© Photo: Marcus Gaab

Studio Hausen • Ringer lounge chair
Prototype
Client: De La Espada
© Studio Hausen

Studio Hausen • Newton lounge chair
Prototype
© Studio Hausen

Camp • Prototypes
'Prototypes' exhibition, Tokyo, 2007
© Takumi Ota

Asterisk Studio • 270° Low / Side / Shelf
'Prototypes' exhibition, Tokyo, 2007
© Takumi Ota

Asterisk Studio • Rebis rocker
'Prototypes' exhibition, Tokyo, 2007
© Takumi Ota

Clemens Weisshaar and Reed Kram • Vendôme
Parametrically designed family of objects
© Kram/Weisshaar

Raphaël von Allmen • Plastic Back chair
Prototype
© ECAL
Photo: Florian Joye

Fernando and Humberto Campana • TransRock chair
© Estúdio Campana

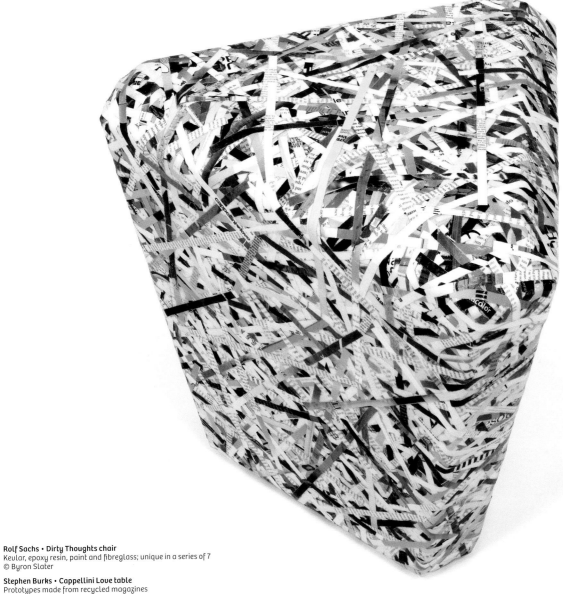

A prototype is a step in the design process. It can stop there, but if it does it means that it has failed. In order to be successful, a prototype has to be followed by industrial development or multiple editions.
Pierre Keller

Rolf Sachs • Dirty Thoughts chair
Kevlar, epoxy resin, paint and fibreglass; unique in a series of 7
© Byron Slater

Stephen Burks • Cappellini Love table
Prototypes made from recycled magazines
Client: Cappellini

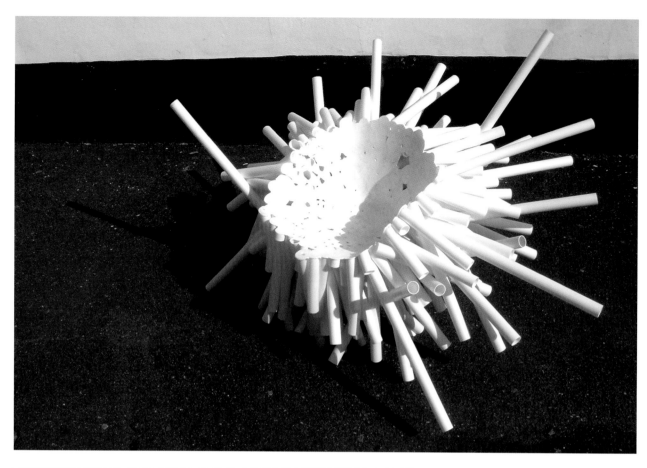

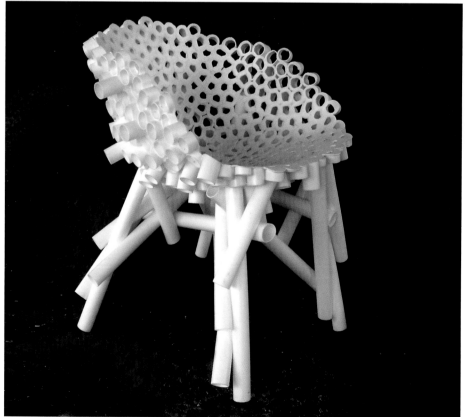

Tom Price • Meltdown chair: PP Tube #1
© Tom Price

Tom Price • Meltdown chair: PP Tube #2
© Tom Price

Tom Price • Meltdown chair: PVC Hose
© Tom Price

Tom Price • Meltdown chair: PP Blue Rope
© Tom Price

These ideas would be the equivalent of, let's say, sketches. They are articulated but not resolved, because they don't need to be – they are not like a vacuum cleaner, they don't need to do anything.
Murray Moss

Kiki van Eijk • Soft cabinet, small
Textiles and ceramics
© Frank Tielemans

Wouter Nieuwendijk and Suzanne van Oirschot • 2D furniture
© Wouter Nieuwendijk

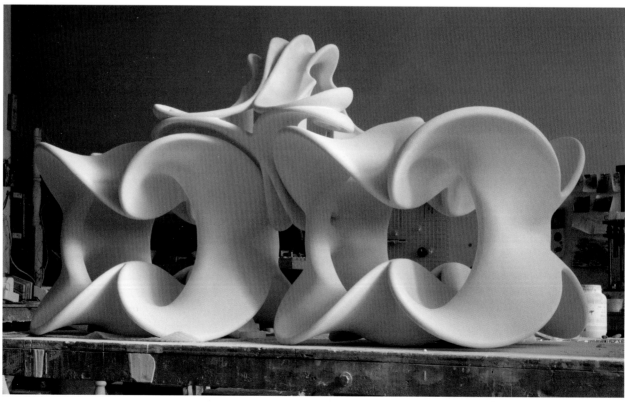

Evan Douglis • Flora_flex
Prototypes
© Evan Douglis

The computer
has revolutionised
the prototyping
process, but it cannot
replace the physical
prototype.

Studio Hausen

In our increasingly standardised global village – where a shopping mall in Auckland can look remarkably similar to a shopping mall in Copenhagen, Dubai or Seville, where we all keep our books on Billy shelves and watch TV from Klippan sofas – a touch of handmade individuality is starting to become rather precious again. Terms such as 'bespoke', 'limited edition', 'unique' and 'handmade' designate a new kind of luxury, where value goes beyond expensive materials and a particular company logo. Consumers also increasingly want products with a story. They want to know who made what they are buying, how it was made and what materials or resources were used in the process. 'People are getting tired of mass-produced products that all look the same and that everybody else has got as well,' say Lisa Widén and Anna Irinarchos from WIS Design. 'Where are the soul and heart in these things? Where are the individuality and the history?'

This desire for additional 'content' in the form of narrative seems to be a growing phenomenon that is beginning to transcend fashion. Narrative can come as performance or documentation, or be inherent within the object itself. A sense of individuality and history can come from the patina of an object that is old and well-worn, or the marks and traces of the maker's hands and tools on something new. It does not necessarily have to start out unique, but it can become so by acquiring a history of its own. 'We are surrounded by man-made objects,' says designer Satyendra Pakhalé. 'They should feel like companions and have a personality and some kind of emotional attachment.' In the case of a handmade piece of furniture for example, the implication is that if the maker has put time, effort and perhaps even love into the making of it, then the later owner will get some of that back from the piece, as well as investing his or her own input into it.

Martino Gamper • '100 Chairs in 100 Days exhibition', 2007
100 unique examples made from re-appropriated found and
donated chairs of all types
Gallery: Nilufar
© Angus Mill

It could be that we are seeking some kind of cultural connection again. Being part of a throwaway society that has also developed through computer use into a magpie culture — indiscriminately appropriating, hybridising and sampling — might mean that we feel left with nothing to hold on to. Objects with stories are like heirlooms; they give us a sense of time beyond ourselves and our place in the order of things. The recent interest in hybridised objects made from old furniture or old forms cut up and remixed like a Moby song reflects this magpie attitude, and a desire for more cultural content that goes beyond nostalgia. 'Handmade objects,' says UK furniture designer Matthew Hilton, 'are artisanal. From the hand and the heart, they are down to earth, the most basic of all objects. They are made the way they have been for millennia.'

But before we put one-offs on a pedestal, we need to remember that unique or handmade objects comprise just a tiny fraction of the realm of design. Mass production is still essential for the needs of mass populations, and most designers still work in this area. An important development, however, is a growing element of choice. Just as consumers can decide whether to spend their money on a cheap set of chairs from one manufacturer, an expensive set from another, commission them from an individual maker, or buy them second-hand, designers are not limited to having to choose between working exclusively in CAD programmes for the mass market or chiselling out every new piece with their own hands. Stephen Burks is a product designer well known for his high-volume work with companies such as Cappellini and B&B Italia, yet he considers unique and what he terms 'artisanal' productions, along with craft traditions, to be an invaluable part of his creative output and development. 'I think in this very pluralistic design moment, there is room for every type of expression. In working more by hand we are reminded of the connection between the hand, the eye and the imagination. I firmly believe that the closer you get to the reality of the materials and the processes of production, the better you can design for them.'

WIS Design produce one-off objects in order to exhibit and illustrate their style. 'When making these objects we don't really have to consider the limitations of mass production. We are quite free in our design process. We can develop the items into objects that could be suitable for the production line later.' Choosing whether to make a piece as a one-off, limited edition, or series of thousands is not of primary concern for many designers. The process and the materials are of interest, rather than the product. For example, Stephen Burks recently took an interest in revisiting various techniques for recycling paper and glass that ended up as a new commercially produced series called Cappellini Love (see page 57). The process started off as a materials experiment and ended up as a product — not the other way around. He did not set out to make tables and vases for Cappellini; he wanted to find a way of re-using the stacks of old magazines in his studio.

Handmade things are artisanal, from the hand and the heart, down to earth, the most basic of all objects.
Matthew Hilton

Max Lamb • Nanocrystalline copper stool
Edition of 1
© Max Lamb

Max Lamb • Ladycross sandstone chair
Edition of 1
© Max Lamb

Max Lamb • Bronze Poly Chair
Unique piece from a series of 10
© Max Lamb

Max Lamb • Poly Chair, bronze + white versions
Edition of 20
© Max Lamb

Many contemporary designers seem to think of themselves as explorers, testing the boundaries of materials, process and medium. The product almost seems to be an afterthought or an added extra. 'You need to be a material scientist,' says designer Gareth Neal. 'You need to experiment and be completely interested in how materials work. Then you also need to be obsessed with the quality of the finish in order to get a product that really sparkles and looks the part. So you have to have a bit of the craftsman in you and a bit of the designer in you as well.' With their one-off experiments, some designers are constantly pushing the envelope. This may or may not result in new or adapted techniques and materials finding their way into the mass market. 'Churning out the same object over and over again is not of interest to me,' says designer Max Lamb. 'I get pleasure from the very experimental stage of developing products and work. I might end up producing just one or two examples of an object and then I'm on to the next project.'

In the furniture world, there have always been designers or artisans who choose to create and develop their own individual pieces on a small scale, often spurning the mainstream and working to commission or selling direct to the customer. It is the way furniture used to be made. If you needed a new table you went to the local carpenter or cabinet maker, told him what you wanted and he made you one. You can still do the same today. The difference is, thanks to communications technology you can choose from tens of thousands of 'local' designers to make your new piece of furniture if you wish. This new kind of availability, paired with increased consumer desire for individuality, has opened up whole new areas of opportunity not just for craftspeople but designers as well: especially for those who consider designing and making to be part of one and the same activity. Thus, consumers seeking furniture products that are different, unique or special can find like-minded designers from all over the globe able to make objects for them that fulfil these requirements. Thanks to the way the market is structured, one-offs and their makers are more accessible than ever before.

A paradox exists between a desire for novelty and innovation on the one hand, and a desire for sustainability and quality on the other. It is a clash between rapid turnover and slow values. Since we moved from a 'hands-on' society to a 'time is money' society, the consensus has been that handmade products take too long to make and cater to too few to be a valid alternative to mass production. 'One-off production is definitely time consuming,' says Matthew Hilton, 'but it doesn't necessarily have to be inefficient. In fact it can be very efficient. I think it is generally worth surrounding yourself with higher-quality goods than lower. The lesser-quality things either wear out, or their charm wears away.' For Satyendra Pakhalé, sustainability has less to do with reducing ecological footprints and more to do with great design and quality based on an approach where a lot of time is invested in getting something right. 'For me the most sustainable product is the one which lasts longer, which becomes a part of cultural history. By that I mean a product that really makes sense and has such significance for people that they cherish it and maybe keep it for the rest of their lives – for generations even – if it is very good.'

For a product to last longer, it needs better quality in design, materials and craftsmanship. Over the course of the late twentieth century, the word 'craft' came to be something of a dirty word in design circles. It smacked of amateur dabbling and hobby practitioners turning out clumsy hand-thrown pots and macramé plant holders. Craft was reduced to a kind of occupational therapy practised by many and mastered by few. But now one begins to hear the term used in a far more positive sense. 'Until recently,' says designer/craftsman Khai Liew, 'design has always evoked the idea of mass production, so anything associated with the word "craft" was not applicable to the design consciousness.' Since the borders began shifting between disciplines and approaches, craft has been accepted back into the design process alongside all the industrial techniques, both old and new, such as vacuum moulding, CNC milling and stereo lithography. In an era where anything goes in the pursuit of the new and the different, nothing is now considered to be incongruous. 'At the beginning of my career,' says Dutch designer Richard Hutten, 'when we first showed our work with Droog design, it was considered to have "too much craft" and not be suitable for mass production. This disadvantage has turned into an advantage over the years.'

Charlie Davidson • Black-Light
Aluminium foil, stainless steel and coloured lighting gels;
individually handmade by Charlie Davidson
© Toby Summerskill

Charlie Davidson • Crunk Chair
Aluminium foil, polyeurethane foam and MDF;
One of a pair
© Toby Summerskill

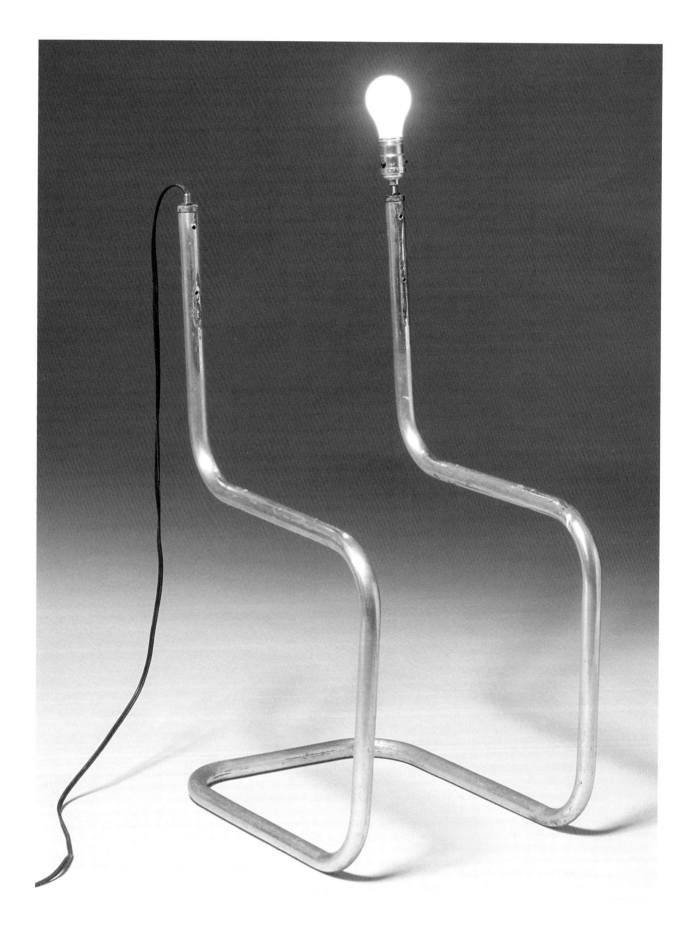

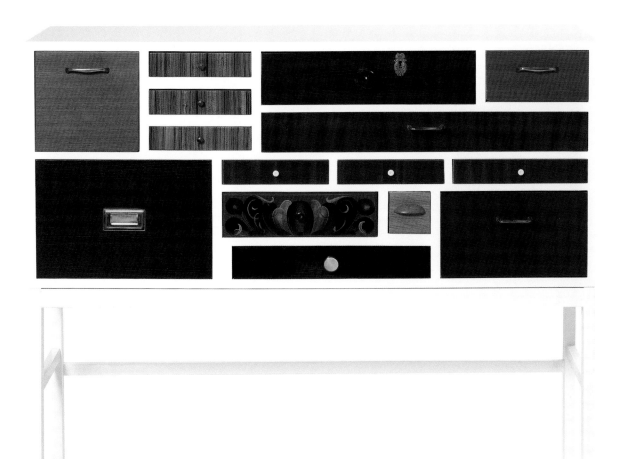

Gord Peteran • Electric Chair
Client: Dr David Dorenbaum
© Elaine Brodie

WIS Design • Decades chest of drawers
© Studio CA

By bringing craft back into their work, these designers are not taking some kind of idealist or Luddite path. There is no hint of rejection of technology in what they are doing. On the contrary, machines and computers are essential – but not necessarily used where one would expect them. When Gareth Neal (see page 74) made his first Anne table, he designed it on the computer but built and cut the whole thing out by hand on a bench saw, because he could not afford to pay for CNC milling. Through the process of making it by hand, accidents occurred and bits of the wood broke off. This inspired him in the making of the next piece, the George 3 console table. This time he could afford the CNC milling, which meant that all the grooves and slots were precision-cut by computer, but he still did all the final abrasion and erosion by hand with a mallet and chisel.

Switching from hand to machine when making limited editions or one-offs rarely means that the products get cheaper, because the quantity is not there to offset the costs. Neal's first method was time-consuming and therefore expensive in labour terms, but the second method is just as expensive, if not more so, because the set-up costs for the machines are so high. Pieces resulting from both processes are equally valuable in his view. To quote Max Lamb again: 'Certainly there's a strong market for unique or customised objects, even if they're produced by a machine. One-off objects that are industrially produced but tweaked in a way that makes them unique are still going to be very expensive, because you're paying for an idea or a concept and for the programme that had to be written which allows each one to be tweaked slightly. It's almost like you're paying for the licence.'

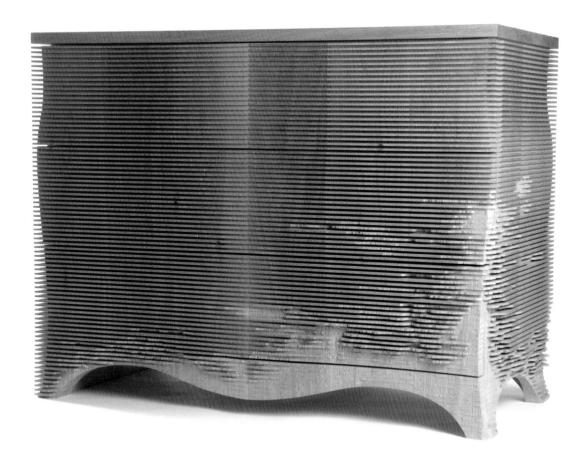

Gareth Neal • George chest of drawers
Oak; edition of 25
© Jim Champion

Khai Liew • Portia
© Grant Hancock

Khai Liew • Linenfold
© Grant Hancock

During the course of his postgraduate education at the Royal College of Art in London, Max Lamb turned away from designing for mass production because he felt he was not able to design commercially viable products. He decided to go back to learning the basics, starting with the very traditional industrial process of sand casting to make a new series of metal furniture. Instead of handing over the production to a factory, Lamb went to a beach and tried it out himself. 'Where I failed at university originally,' he explains, 'is that I was designing function and designing objects that sold function in clever ways. But when it came to the actual manufacture and selling I went wrong because I wasn't designing objects that could be made very successfully.' So he decided to start learning all about materials and processes first, and only then to design objects around them. 'That is the only real way to design and produce objects that you are ultimately going to be able to make and sell,' he adds. In switching from a theory-led approach to a craft and hands-on approach, Lamb's move is exemplary of a shift in the modern product design paradigm. He bypassed expensive tooling and manufacturing limitations, created a unique piece of furniture, gave it narrative by documenting the process, and made it work commercially. His failings as an industrial designer have proved to be his strengths as a designer/maker. He has found his product and his market and proved that less can most definitely be more. Lamb's gallery, the Johnson Trading Gallery, recently sold a set of his Bronze Poly chairs (see page 69) at the 2008 Design Miami/Basel for $25,000 a piece.

Admittedly, Max Lamb's success story will not happen to every designer/maker out there – and his strategy is by no means unique either. But it is a rather good example that illustrates well the flexibility of the contemporary design path. Craft, skill, culture, process, materials, tools and communications technology as well as manufacturing technology can all be mixed and remixed in an extraordinary variety of ways. There is also an increasingly design-aware and critical market out there, with buyers getting tired of being dictated to by an old industrially driven system that has been superseded by a new reality.

Until recently, design has always evoked the idea of mass production, so anything associated with the word 'craft' was not applicable to the design consciousness. The borders are currently shifting and craft in design is regarded in a more positive manner.

Khai Liew

I think we have a natural connection to things made by hand. People talk of the "individuality" and imperfections which mark objects made by hand and make them special.

but the difference between something which has these marks of individuality of making and is beautiful because of them and something bearing these marks and being just badly made is very, very subtle.

Matthew Hilton

Ayala Serafaty (Aqua Creations) • Soma / Memory lamps
Gallery: Aqua Gallery
© Albi Serafaty

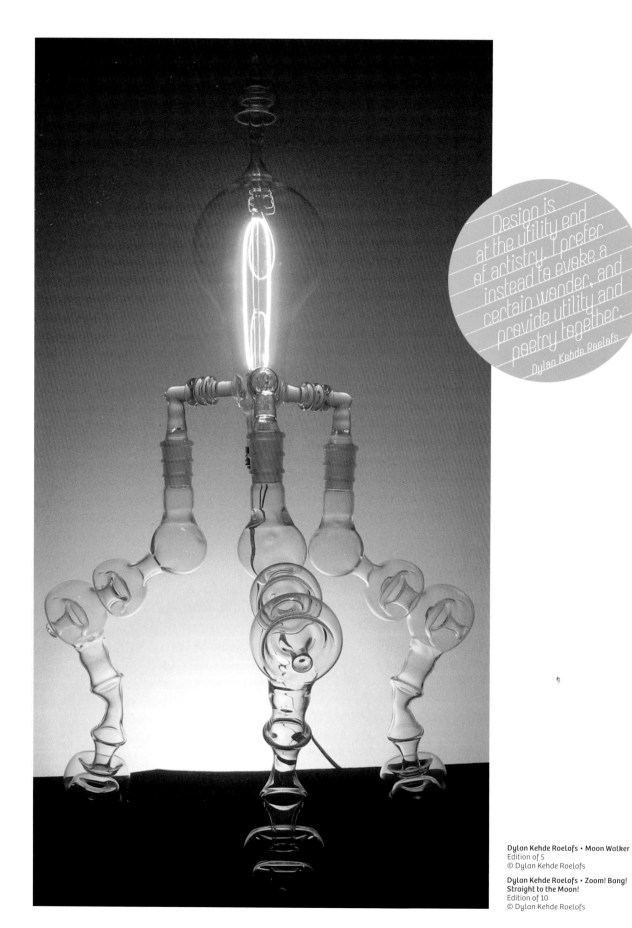

Design is at the utility end of artistry. I prefer instead to evoke a certain wonder, and provide utility and poetry together.
Dylan Kehde Roelofs

Dylan Kehde Roelofs • Moon Walker
Edition of 5
© Dylan Kehde Roelofs

Dylan Kehde Roelofs • Zoom! Bang! Straight to the Moon!
Edition of 10
© Dylan Kehde Roelofs

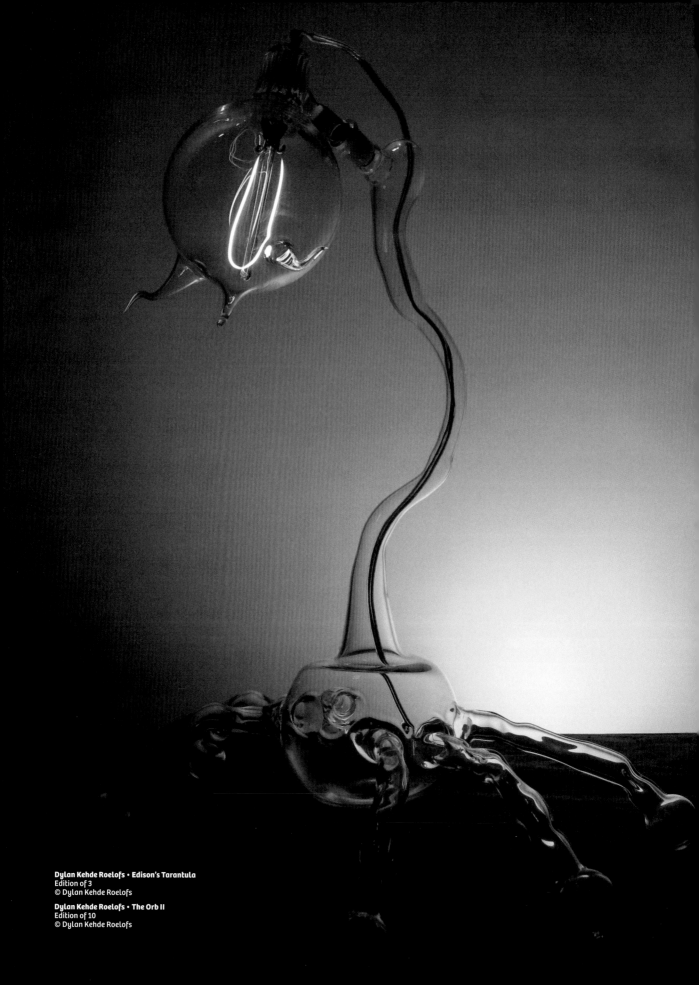

Lonneke Gordijn for Drift • Fragile Future
Modular light system; electronics, phosphorus bronze, LED lights, dandelion seed heads
© Design Drift

Gord Peteran • Early Table
From the 'Demi-Lune' series of one-offs
Client: William Anderson
© Elaine Brodie

Gord Peteran • Suspended Table
From the 'Demi-Lune' series of one-offs
Client: William Anderson
© Elaine Brodie

Gord Peteran • A Table Made of Wood
The first table of the 'Demi-Lune' series of one-offs
© Elaine Brodie

Gord Peteran • A Table Made of Wood
From the 'Demi-Lune' series of one-offs
Client: Richard Ivy
© Elaine Brodie

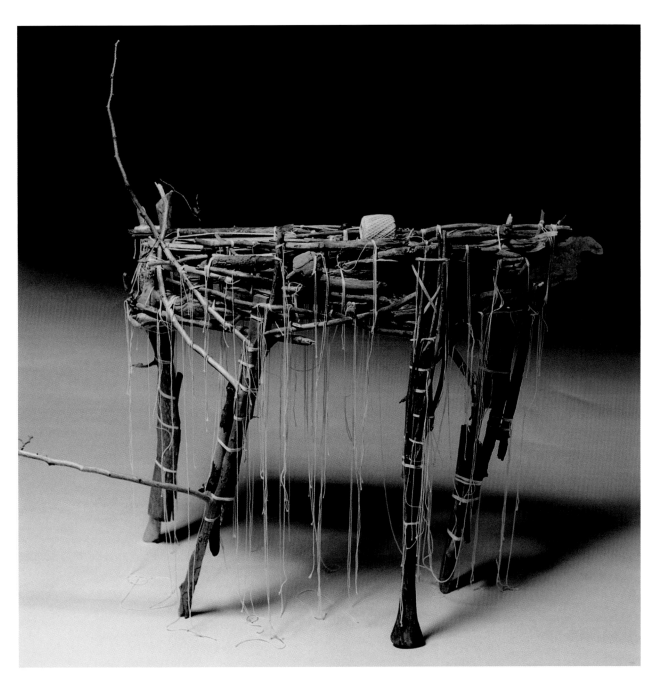

Gord Peteran • Study Station
© Elaine Brodie

Diego Ramos and Luis Eslava • Tyvek World
One-off objects made from Tyvek polyethylene fibre material
© Vanessa Moreno

I think designers are responding to the consumer and the market, and that's definitely changed.

Rather than the homogenised, globalised high street, which is international, people want something which they feel is truly personalised, and I think that's what this market or this agenda is going for or trying to satisfy.
Libby Sellers

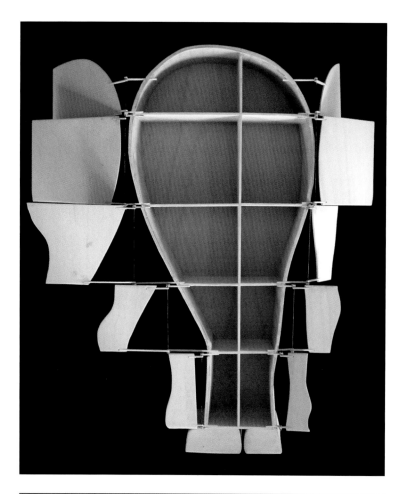

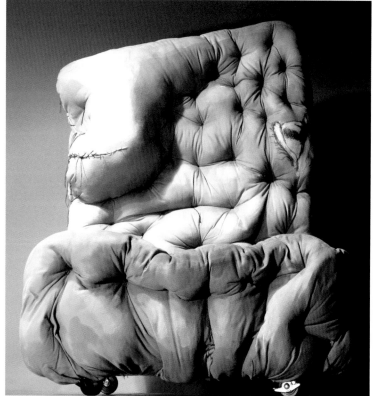

Gaetano Pesce • Horse Cabinet
One-off
© Gaetano Pesce

Anna Blattert, Daniel Gafner (Postfossil) • First Light
Reading lamp powered mechanically by weight and cog wheels
like a grandfather clock mechanism
© Postfossil

Gaetano Pesce • Poltrona Naso chair
One-off
© Gaetano Pesce

Graham Hudson • History is cheap
Gallery: Rokeby
© Graham Hudson; Rokeby Gallery

Every object takes time to arrive. Labour is the same. Too much and too little is noticeable.

A certain amount of resistance is required for the object to last, to endure, to sustain. This goes for both the maker and the client. For the commitment to remain there needs to be evidence of significant investment.

It has to hurt a little. This can come in many forms. One is the marks of the hand. Another is the marks left from extended cerebral rigour. Another is simply the passing of time.
Gord Peteran

Freshwest Design • **Brave New World coffee table**
© Freshwest Design

Frédéric Ruyant • **Reading Cabinet**
Signed series numbered 1 to 50
Gallery: OZZ Gallery
© Frédéric Ruyant Design

Frédéric Ruyant • **Tête à Tête with Oneself**
Signed series numbered 1 to 50
Gallery: OZZ Gallery
© Frédéric Ruyant Design

Frédéric Ruyant • **Tea Pavilion**
Signed series numbered 1 to 50
Gallery: OZZ Gallery
© Frédéric Ruyant Design

Lund University Industrial Design, LTH • What Can You Bring to the Table
One-offs designed by students; each chair component is designed
independently of the others, following an emotional theme
© Jonas Wåglund

**Farmdesign / Guy Brown • School Days collection: Siamese Chair; Cone
Head; Chair Coat Stand; School Chaise**
© Guy Brown

Farmdesign / Guy Brown • Chairs-in-Chairs / Tablelamp
© Guy Brown

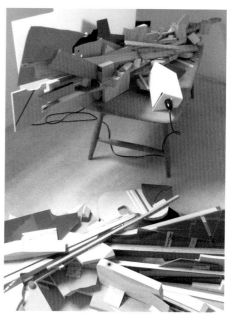

Karen Ryan • Wood Work lights
Gallery: Spazio Rossana Orlandi, Milan
© Karen Ryan

Pieke Bergmanns and Peter van der Jagt • Melted collection
Baked plastic objects
© Studio Design Virus

People are getting tired of mass-produced products that all look the same and that everybody else has got as well. Where is the soul and heart in these products? Where is the individuality, the history?

WIS Design

Martino Gamper • '100 Chairs in 100 Days' exhibition, 2007
Selection from 100 unique examples made from re-appropriated
found and donated chairs of all types
Gallery: Nilufar
© Åbäke

Nacho Carbonell · Evolution
Recycled paper and iron frame
© Nacho Carbonell

Tejo Remy · Tennis Ball bench
Client: Museum Boymans van Beuningen
© Mels v. Zuphten

Tomek Rygalik · Raw leather armchair
'Prototypes & Experiments' exhibition, 2007
Gallery: The Aram Gallery
© Tomek Rygalik

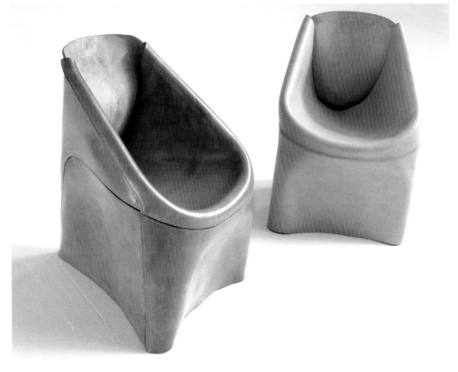

Tomás Alonso • 5 Degree Stool
© Tomás Alonso

Oscar Magnus Narud • Side table
One-off
© Oscar Narud

Oscar Magnus Narud • Vault chair
One-off
© Oscar Narud

Oscar Magnus Narud • Pick-A-Stick
One-off
© Oscar Narud

Peter Marigold • Octave series
Edition of 12
Gallery: Gallery Libby Sellers
© Peter Marigold

Handmade furniture objects are not elitist, but they are a luxury.
Helen Amy Murray

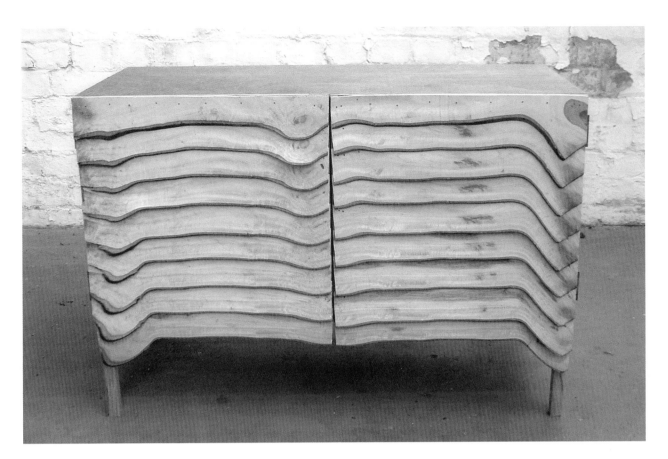

Piet Hein Eek • Kitchen Cupboard
© Nob Ruijgrok

Peter Marigold • Thin Slice cabinet
One-off
Gallery: Gallery Libby Sellers
© Peter Marigold

Winnie Lui • White chandelier
Client: Innermost
Gallery: Spazio Rossana Orlandi, Milan
© Rachel Smith

Winnie Lui • Black chandelier
Client: Innermost
Gallery: Spazio Rossana Orlandi, Milan
© Until Chan

Pieke Bergmans • Massive Infection
Presented by Droog Design
© Studio Design Virus

Pieke Bergmans • Crystal Virus
Handmade series produced with Royal Crystal Leerdam. Clients
are required to go and watch their own pieces being made.
© Studio Design Virus

Pieke Bergmans • Crystal Virus
© Studio Design Virus

Pieke Bergmans & Madieke Fleuren • Unlimited Edition
Unlimited edition of unique pieces produced by extruding clay
into tubes and deforming when wet
© Studio Design Virus

Pieke Bergmans • Light Blub
From a series of unique hand-crafted crystal pieces with LEDs
designed in co-operation with Royal Crystal Leerdam
© Studio Design Virus

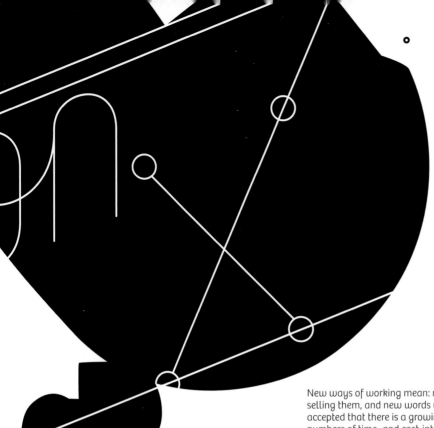

New ways of working mean: new categories of products, new ways of selling them, and new words with which to talk about them. It is generally accepted that there is a growing branch of design that generates small numbers of time- and cost-intensive objects, whose primary purpose is not necessarily functional. Whether this kind of design is 'new' in itself, whether it represents a movement, a fashion fad or, in some cases, a type of art, is still a matter of debate.

Alexander Payne, director of design at Phillips de Pury & Company auction house, is generally credited with coining the contemporary use of the term 'Design Art' back in 1999. 'I used the terminology back at the turn of the millennium to create a provocative and interesting concept for people to discuss and debate,' he says. 'It was very interesting to look at how design and art and architecture were fusing and melding into this one language and barriers were being broken down, lines were being blurred.' However, what seems to have been a reasonable attempt to put a name to this type of furniture design, so that buyers and sellers knew what they were talking about, ended up causing such a stink amongst artists, designers, gallerists, collectors and, most notably, the media, that Payne publicly retracted the term in early 2008.

The issue people have with the expression 'Design Art' seems to have less to do with the question of what is 'art' and what is 'design', and more to do with a commercially driven interest in giving kudos to the designer-produced furniture market by appropriating the word 'art'. It is true that over the past decade or so contemporary design objects have begun to appear in contexts previously reserved for art: in galleries, at art auctions, at art fairs, on pedestals and in white spaces. But since art itself survives and thrives amidst the dirty machinations of commerce without apparently losing its credibility, it is hard to see what all the fuss is about.

Arguing the point in the other direction by saying that adding the word 'Art' after 'Design' somehow negates the value or meaning of design is slightly more interesting. But the idea that design should have a primary utilitarian responsibility, and that without this functional role it is diminished and therefore bad in some way, is a rather dated and utopian mid-twentieth-century view. The real difficulty critics have with the term 'Design Art' is that collectors are attracted to this new kind of design so much that they are prepared to spend very large sums of money on it. Prices are climbing and the market is growing, which must mean that 'Design Art' is important. But is it important like a piece by, say, Marcel Duchamp or Neo Rauch? Does it push boundaries or express the zeitgeist? Or is it important as a status symbol like a Damien Hirst dot painting or a Ferrari? And is there a difference any more? There is as much bad and overpriced design around as there is bad and overpriced art. Who cares, as long as it sells?

Fredrikson Stallard • King Bonk armchair and stool
Edition of 8, 2 artist's proofs and 2 prototypes
Gallery: David Gill Galleries
© David Gill Galleries
Photo: Thomas Brown

Certainly there is nothing new about edition furniture for those who can afford it. 'Rich people have always bought extraordinary and limited-quantity furniture that was different from what everybody else could have,' says British designer Tom Dixon. 'Whether that was the big decorators of the 1930s working for Maharajahs, or even the Modernists like Le Corbusier, in the end they were making rare things for rich people. Pernette Perriand, the daughter of Charlotte Perriand, told me they only sold around twenty-five of the very famous [B306 Le Corbusier] chaises longues before the war. So those were the kind of quantities that even the most iconic, supposedly mass-produced products were being made in then.' The American designer Johanna Grawunder agrees: 'There has always been limited-edition design. Architects of the past made chairs and sofas and tables for their houses. Look at Hoffmann, Prouvé, Wright, Loos, Ponti, Le Corbusier and so on. Six chairs for a private home is limited edition design, so are twenty-five desks for an office, so it's nothing new.'

In terms of collecting, there are gallerists who have been showing and selling design for decades. A pioneering collector is London's David Gill. In 1987 he opened his first gallery that 'comfortably blurs the boundaries between applied and fine arts'. There, along with art objects, he started showing furniture by people like Charlotte Perriand and Jean Prouvé, before quickly moving on to exhibit early pieces by Tom Dixon, Marc Newson and Ron Arad. Gill has no problem with the design/art comparison. He likens the Prince Imperial chair, designed by Mattia Bonetti and Elizabeth Garouste in 1985, to a Gauguin painting. 'I already saw at this point a crossover between art and design with this piece,' he says.

Going further back to over one hundred years ago, it is also worth remembering that the late nineteenth-century Arts and Crafts movement was all about challenging industrial mores and celebrating the designer craftsman. It was also a reaction to Victorian eclecticism and an 'anything goes' attitude to styles and forms. Although somewhat traditionalist in its principles, the movement still rejected historicism and generated small quantities of furniture pieces that were innovative and experimental, made from fine materials both by hand and machine, that only the lucky few could afford. The twentieth-century tradition of designer-produced furniture objects that hover somewhere along the edge of art, craft, industry and functionality stretches from the tail end of Arts and Crafts through Modernism to the Italian group Memphis in the 1980s and the Dutch group Droog Design in the 1990s, right up to the present day. What they all have in common is a sense of exploration and experimental innovation that challenges preconceived forms and materials in design.

The Design Art/Limited Edition market exists as a laboratory, a place where things can be worked on and developed that might get stuck in 'development hell' if they were handed over to the big design companies.
Nick Compton

It would be absurd to look at a Campana chair now and go: 'How comfortable is that, and will it blend me in with my sofa?'

absurd not because one shouldn't ask those things about sofas or chairs, but because it's absurd to ask that about this chair.

Murray Moss

With the increasing volume and value of the art market, this furniture somehow slipped into the role of being an art accessory at first, and then acquired a market in its own right. Perhaps it is now time for critics to talk about more than just the price tag and whether we should call it 'art' or not. An appropriate terminology is essential if we are to discuss what is happening to design – and yet we are still trapped in a dated vocabulary. Wava Carpenter, Director of Culture and Content for the Design Miami/Basel fair, agrees: 'One of the biggest challenges facing design practice today is the problem of semantics. We lack consensus on the meaning and connotations of the words we use to categorise work under the umbrella of "design". On the one hand this is a good problem to have, because it results from the tremendous proliferation of approaches, tools, techniques, theoretical foundations, marketplaces and applications for design thinking available to today's designers. On the other hand it generates confusion that hampers discourse.'

A term that is increasingly used to cover new and experimental design work is 'Limited-Edition Design'. The word 'edition' comes from art. It originally meant a restricted number of impressions taken from the printed surface when making a print of an image. Artists tend to make one-offs, but if something proves popular they may make an edition of it. Photographs tend to be in editions too, as do, on occasion, sculptural pieces. In order avoid flooding the market and to maintain value, editions are limited traditionally to anything between two and one thousand. Each is signed, numbered and dated by the artist: all value-enhancing measures. The smaller the number of the edition, the more valuable the pieces are, because they are closer to being unique. Thus, by calling new design objects 'Limited Edition' we are classifying them in an art context just as strongly as when we call them 'Design Art'. If we wanted to stay closer to the design aspect, the experimental nature of the work and perhaps vestiges of function without attempting to assign value, then perhaps 'Prototype Design' or 'Experimental Design' would fit better – but those names don't sound nearly as alluring or exclusive.

XYZ Design • Fake
Series of 20 one-offs
Gallery: Contrasts Gallery
© Contrasts Gallery
Photo: Julian de Hauteclocque Howe

Tom Dixon • CU29 Chair
Edition of 8
© Tom Dixon Studio

Carpenter advocates using the term 'Limited-Edition Design' because, she explains, it 'represents progress towards clarity by denoting any type of design object produced outside of the industrial system, encompassing the relatively small portion of design work that explores experimental, not-yet-mass-produceable processes, or revisits craft or hand processes, or incorporates rare and unusual materials'. This term fits well with the majority of work represented in this book, but we need to guard against using it too broadly. 'As a definition, the suggestion of Limited Edition is close,' says Libby Sellers, a gallerist and former curator of London's Design Museum. She uses it to describe the field she works in: 'Giving young designers a platform to show new work' as well as the work of more established big name designers. But she also adds that it would be 'completely inappropriate' to use this definition for vintage pieces from the likes of Jean Prouvé and Alvar Aalto, 'because they were not made as design art at the time but for schools and hospitals or whatever'. Clearly, an introspective exploration of the materiality and process of the object itself has to play a role in limited-edition design. It sets itself apart from work that is primarily site- or function-specific.

Sellers is also very cautious about labelling in general. Names and categories may encourage debate, but they can also be damaging. She cites the term 'Dubai Chic' coined by David Carlson of David Design in Sweden. 'Comments like that make me very anxious,' says Sellers. 'They create the bandwagon and the hype which could unfortunately lead to the downfall of the market. I think that is why most of us feel awkward about trying to put a label on it, because it means so many things to so many different people.'

The designers making these limited-edition pieces are surprisingly unanimous about what creating in this area means from their point of view: freedom. 'As an industrial designer,' says Marc Newson, 'I work to briefs, but in the case of my limited-edition works I have none, so I can create my own parameters. I can let my imagination run free and express my enthusiasm for materials, processes and techniques – but on my terms.' Tom Dixon, an equally experienced and established designer, echoes his sentiments. 'When I started off,' he says, 'I wasn't thinking of my work as limited edition. It was limited by the fact that it was made with found objects, so it was impossible to make the same piece twice. I was limited by circumstance, really.' Dixon later went on to work very successfully in the realm of industrial design, but has grasped the opportunity that this new interest in limited editions has created. 'I think I've taken full advantage of the market changing to do exactly what I was before, but in a slightly more attractive way. I'm using it as somewhere I can experiment rather than trying to make everything work from a commerce view. It gives you a space to be much more daring if you like.'

Designers from the Droog generation talk not only about experiment, but about theory and research as well. Hella Jongerius calls her limited-edition pieces 'study cases'. For her they are new ideas that have no client in mind, no market and no industrial restrictions. 'I have been making these self-initiated projects right from the start,' she says, 'partly because I didn't have any clients at the beginning and also because with these study objects you build up a library of ideas that you can use later for real clients.' Jongerius is at pains to point out that she is not interested in 'just making stupid things for the money'. She thought twice, for example, when Vitra asked her to make something for their 2007 collection entitled 'Vitra Edition'. 'I asked them: "Why should I do limited editions for you when you are already my client and we make nice products together anyway?"' She resolved the issue by making a collection of strange objects on wheels called 'office pets' that are a study about the nature of Vitra as a company and what they make: office systems and office chairs. 'I'm trying to push the boundaries of my profession,' concludes Jongerius, 'and my profession is making functional pieces for a market. I'm trying to come up with new ideas for this machinery, to search for a new grammar in my field.'

Laurent Massaloux • Vanitytidy XL
Gallery: ToolsGalerie
© Marc Domage

François Brument and Ammer Eloueini • Chair #71
Edition of 3
© Véronique Huygue

The edition work, by eliminating most of the constraints, can trigger something surprising and, with a lot of effort and luck, something beautiful that – with even more luck – later leads to a new approach to an everyday problem.
Rolf Fehlbaum

Jurgen Bey, another Dutch designer, compares what is happening at the moment with design to a phase in Dutch architecture in the 1980s: 'Architects had this great moment of evolving when they could hardly build anything. This was a paper architecture period where architects wrote a lot and developed incredible model-making. Koolhaas was making all these models that were quite abstract, expressions – almost like art. I think design also needs this period. Not that we shouldn't be making things, but in the sense of finding a way to develop its course. We need good debate. Limited edition gives you the opportunity to do something that otherwise you'd never have the chance to do. There is more money to be spent, so you can investigate a lot more, and I think that is a very good reason to do it. But within the way you work, you also have responsibilities: towards yourself and where you stand, for instance. As a studio, we do limited editions and spend a lot of money on them. Some projects are underpaid, some are overpaid. We do these things because it makes it possible to develop an academic way of working within a studio.' Both Bey and Jongerius view limited-edition design as part of a much bigger picture. It represents products and ideas from the research departments of their studios – real prototype design – but is never the be-all and end-all of their professions.

A third Dutch designer, a young star of the scene Maarten Baas, only makes limited-edition pieces. But this, he says, is because he is a hands-on designer/producer and therefore has purely practical reasons. 'I don't set out to make anything as limited edition. I know that is what some designers do, but I don't believe in it. My things are expensive to make and I don't have enough people to make a hundred copies, so I limit them because I have no other choice... Limited editions, the way that I see them, are things you put a lot of effort into and really want to make the best out of. If I felt I could not add something to what is there already, then I would maybe get sick of it. With everything I make I think, "this should really be in the world because I believe in it". I feel a really deep essence [sic] to do it.'

Of course there are designers, dealers and companies out there producing limited-edition objects with the exclusive aim of cashing in on a fashion. The idea of doing a gold-plated version of some well-known or innovative object and making just eight copies to sell directly at auction is widespread, and there are plenty of individuals with large wallets who are prepared to buy them. At worst, as Libby Sellers fears, they are destroying the market, but at best they are encouraging the injection of capital into a phase of conceptual exploration in the design world. With or without the bad-taste bling, there are enough designers involved in this exploration to be able to say that what we are witnessing is far more than just a trend. 'It is not a fashion,' says designer Philip Michael Wolfson, 'but a more tactile awareness of how we operate in the space around us. It is part of this 3D awakening that is becoming a more predominant symbol of contemporary society.'

To me [Design Art is] a bastardisation. There's design and there's design and art and there's design can be marketed via design editions like art, but limited editions like art, but it's not an appropriate term to use.

James Zemaitis

Fredrikson Stallard • Rubber table
Edition of 8, 2 artist's proofs and 2 prototypes
Gallery: David Gill Galleries
© David Gill Galleries
Photo: Gareth Hacker

Johanna Grawunder • Angel corner cabinet
Mirror, Macassar wood, glass and fluorescent light; edition of 4
Gallery: Galleria Roberto Giustini & Partners
© Neubauten Studio

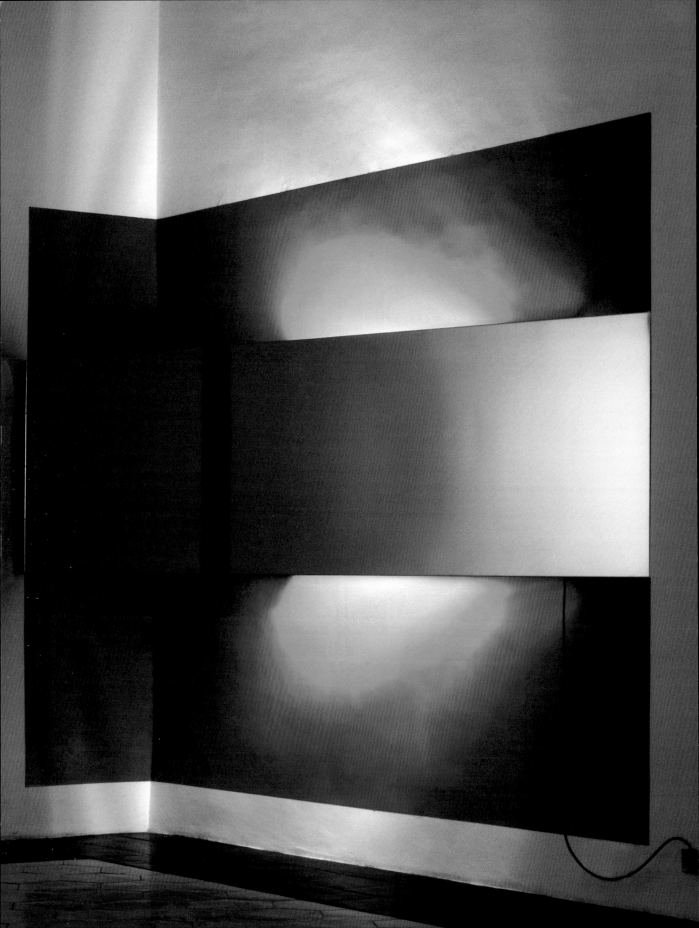

Johanna Grawunder • Trave
Wall-mounted console; edition of 4
Gallery: Galleria Roberto Giustini & Partners
© Neubauten Studio

Martino Gamper • Corner Totem
Edition of 12
Gallery: Nilufar
© Martino Gamper

Martino Gamper • Sit Together Bench
Edition of 12
Gallery: The Aram Gallery
© Anne Hardy

Even from a manufacturer's point of view, limited-edition design can be liberating and regenerating – in small doses. 'To change the criteria can lead to interesting results,' says Rolf Fehlbaum, CEO of Vitra. 'In the usual design process you work with many constraints: price, functions, ecology, ergonomics etc. These constraints are nothing to complain about; finding solutions for them is in the very nature of design. However, constraints often censor new ideas. By eliminating most of them, edition work can trigger something surprising and, with a lot of effort and luck, something beautiful and, with even more luck, something that later leads to a new approach to an everyday problem.'

Limited-edition design really does mean so many things to so many different people. It is no wonder that debate has been slow in coming and that consensus over definitions is hard to achieve. For some it is design; for others, it's art. It is both serious research and creative expression; it is investment, both conceptual and financial; and at its worst it is trophies and fashion, price tags and status symbols. Ideally, as an experimental and exploratory form that is part of a bigger picture, limited edition will end up demonstrating its greatest value. As Jurgen Bey so aptly puts it: 'When you want to progress, you should develop in all fields, on all levels, in everything. There's creative development, technographic development and there's social behaviour development and social intelligence. I think it's important to grow in all of them, because with them culture grows, and culture is the highest art form that we have.'

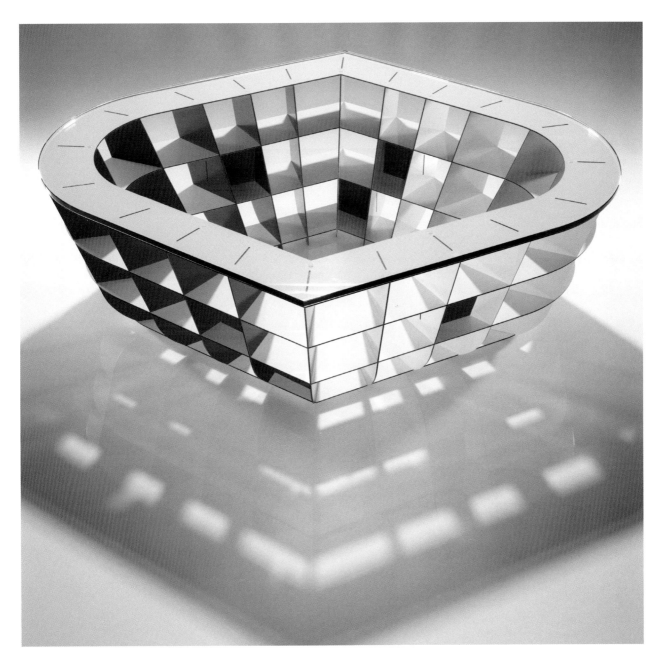

Maarten Baas · Sculpt dining chairs, black + stainless steel
Editions of 8 and 2 artist's proofs
© Maarten van Houten

Maarten Baas · Sculpt drawer, black
Edition of 8 and 2 artist's proofs
© Maarten van Houten

Laurent Massaloux · Ribbedred
Gallery: ToolsGalerie
© Daniel Schweiger

Fredrikson Stallard · Pyrenees Sofa
Edition of 8, 2 artist's proofs and 2 prototypes
Gallery: David Gill Galleries
© David Gill Galleries

I'm not interested in just making in just making stupid things for the money.

Hella Jongerius

Janette Laverrière • Nénuphar Miroir: low table in three parts
Edition of 8, 2 artist's proofs and 2 prototypes
Gallery: Perimeter Editions
© Claude Weber

Olivier Peyricot • HB table
Gallery: ToolsGalerie
© Marc Domage

Richard Hutten • Sexy Relaxy Mirrorsteel chair
Edition of 8
© Richard Hutten Studio

Andrea Salvetti • Joe
Edition of 6 and 3 artist's proofs
Gallery: Nilufar
© Nilufar

As an industrial
designer I work to
briefs, but in the case of
the limited-edition works,
I have none, so I can create my
own parameters. I can let my
imagination run free and express
my enthusiasm for materials,
processes and techniques —
but on my terms.
Marc Newson

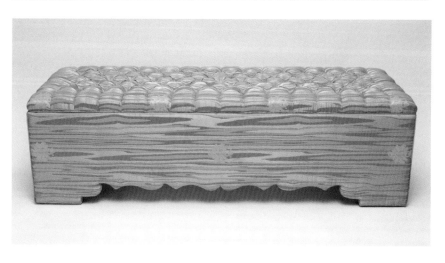

Minale-Maeda • Survival Furniture shelf and chandelier
Wood upholstered in silk brocade;
edition of 5 plus 2 artists' proofs each
Gallery: Droog Design; ToolsGalerie
© Mario Minale

Minale-Maeda • Survival Furniture bench
Wood upholstered in silk brocade;
edition of 5 plus 2 artists' proofs each
Gallery: Droog Design; ToolsGalerie
© Mario Minale

Arik Levy • Cubic Meter
Edition of 12
Gallery: Kenny Schachter ROVE Projects
© Kenny Schachter ROVE Projects

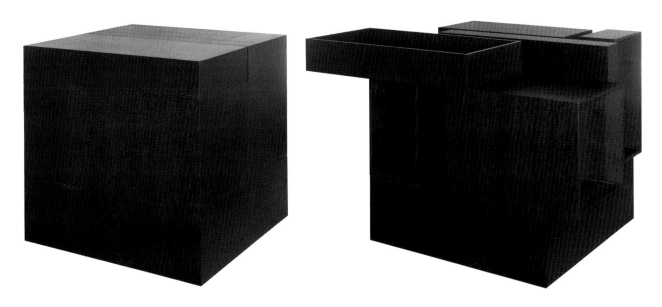

Jeremy Cole · Aloe Blossom lamp
Special gold version in an edition of 500
© Xavier Young

Front · Confetti lamp
Client: BSweden
© Front

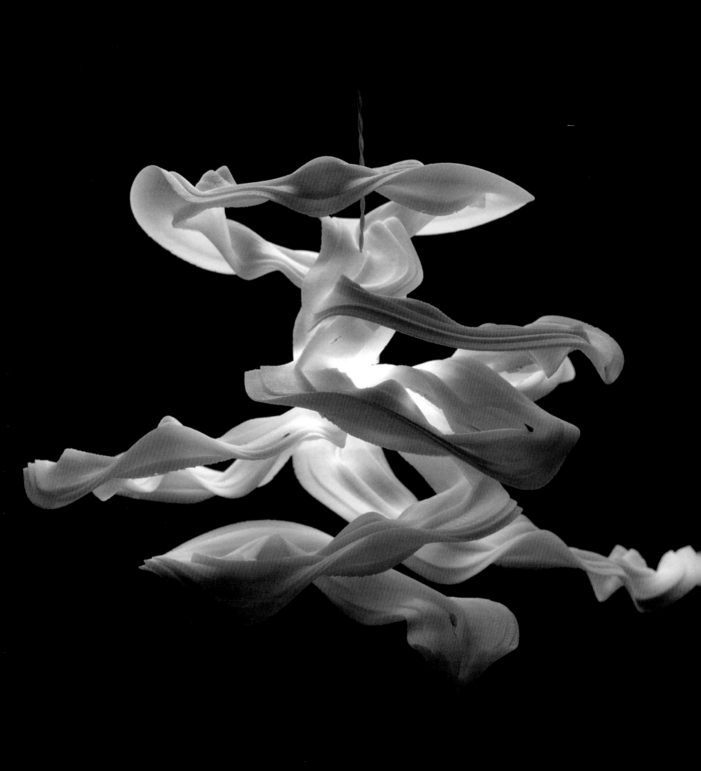

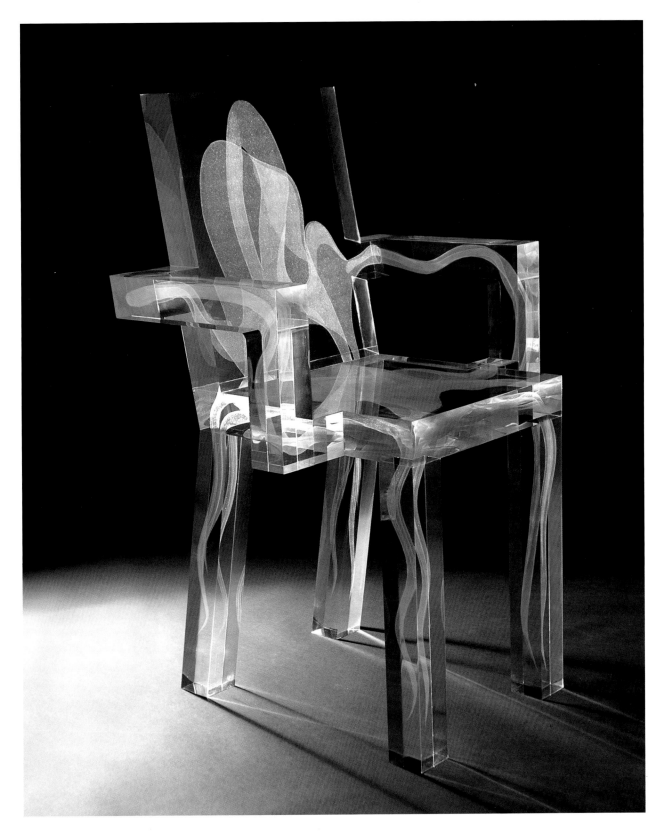

Geoffrey Mann • Attracted to Light
Edition of 5 plus 1 artist's proof
© Sylvain Deleu

Design Drift • Ghost Collection: King Chair
Edition of 8 and 2 artist's proofs
© Design Drift

Gudrun Lilja / Studio Bility • Curiosity Cabinet
Edition of 3 signed pieces and 1 artist's proof
Gallery: ToolsGalerie
© Studio Bility

Martino Gamper • Together bookcase
Edition of 12 and 3 artist's proofs
Gallery: Nilufar
© Nilufar

Matthew Hilton • Wood table
Client: De La Espada
© Matthew Hilton

Tom Dixon • Flame Swing
Edition of 12
© Tom Dixon Studio

Guillaume Bardet • Immobile, Demi Galet table
Edition of 8, 2 prototypes plus 2 artist's proofs
Gallery: Perimeter Editions
© Pierre-Olivier Deschamps

Rolf Sachs • Tailor Made chair
Merino felt; edition of 7
© Byron Slater

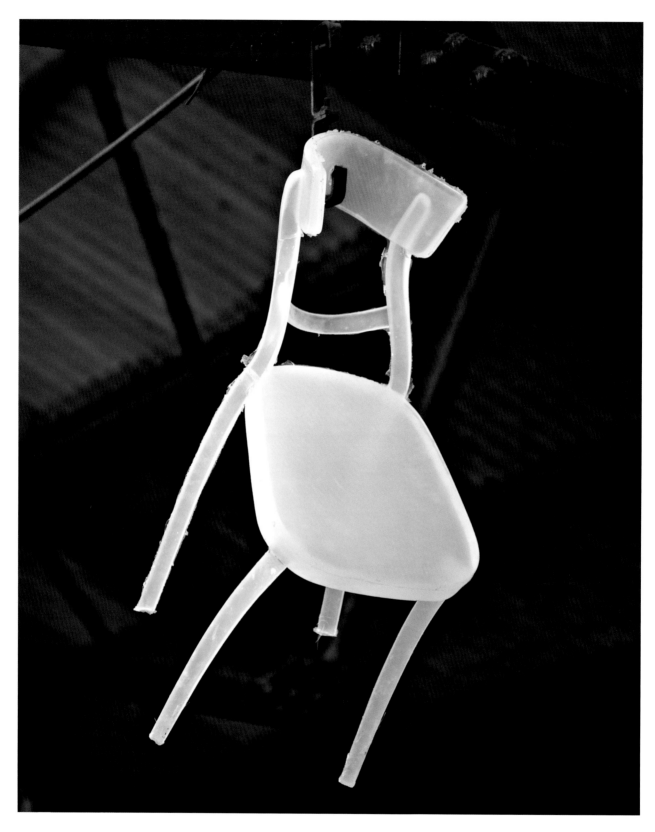

Rolf Sachs · Spineless chair
Edition of 12
© Byron Slater

Rolf Sachs · Spitting Image table and chairs, armchair and chair
Edition of 96
© Byron Slater

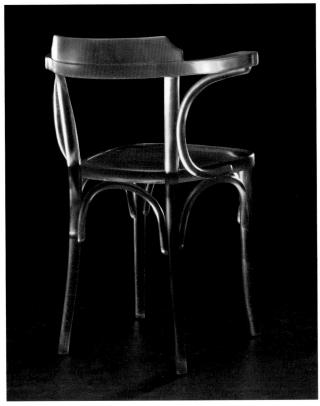

Rick Owens • Curial Chair
Edition of 25 and 2 artist's proofs
Gallery: Jousse Entreprise
© Jousse Entreprise
Photo: Marc Domage

Rick Owens • Gallic Chair
Edition of 20 and 2 artist's proofs
Gallery: Jousse Entreprise
© Jousse Entreprise
Photo: Marc Domage

Stuart Haygarth • Black Millennium
MDF, monofilament line, split shot, 1000 exploded party poppers;
edition of 10
© Stuart Haygarth

Stuart Haygarth • Optical
MDF, monofilament line, split shot, prescription spectacle lenses;
edition of 5 large and 5 small
© Stuart Haygarth

Russell Pinch • Marlow armoire
© Nato Welton

Russell Pinch • Alba armoire
© Nato Welton

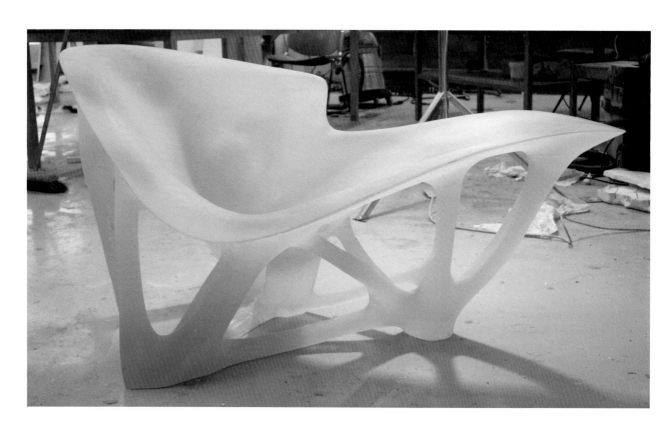

> I try to make my limited pieces really "limited" in that they need so much handwork or they are so strange, that nobody wants them.
>
> Hella Jongerius

Joris Laarman • Bone chaise
Chaise longue in polyurethane-based resin; a computer-generated 'natural' form
© Bas Helbers

XYZ Design • Artwork No. 2
Edition of 20
Gallery: Contrasts Gallery
© Contrasts Gallery

Front • Reflection Cupboard
Gallery: Galerie Kreo
© Front

Front• Reflection Sideboard
Gallery: Galerie Kreo
© Front

When people ask me: "What edition is your work?" I'll say: "It's work, but not an edition, but there's a series of ten of them."

Max Lamb

Studio Job • Pouring Jug
Unique piece
© Z33

Studio Job • Homework
Edition of 6 and 2 artist's proofs
Gallery: Moss New York / Los Angeles
Collection: Groninger Museum
© Z33

Studio Job • Silverware
Edition of 6 and 2 artist's proofs
Collection: Bisazza
© Z33

Studio Job • Paper Furniture
Unique pieces
Collection: Royal Tichelaar Makkum
© Z33

My heart has always been in the limited-edition, one-off, commission-based work, but the reality of this work for a bespoke designer is that when you design something just once the whole time and only make ten of it, there's no serious bread and butter in it unless you start commanding the high prices.

Gareth Neal

Studio Job • Robber Baron cabinet
From a suite of 5 cast-bronze objects, consisting of a cabinet, mantel clock, table, standing lamp and jewel safe, each in a limited edition of 5, and 2 artist's proofs
Gallery: Moss New York / Los Angeles
© Robert Kot, Brussels

Studio Job • Robber Baron jewel safe
From a suite of 5 cast-bronze ojects, consisting of a cabinet, mantel clock, table, standing lamp and jewel safe, each in a limited edition of 5, and 2 artist's proofs
Gallery: Moss New York / Los Angeles
© Robert Kot, Brussels

When I was starting off I wasn't thinking of it as limited edition, it was limited by the very fact that it was made with found objects so in that context it was impossible to make the same one twice. I was limited by circumstance really.

Tom Dixon

Studio Job • Flower Pyramid
Edition of 6 and 2 artist's proofs
Collection: Royal Tichelaar Makkum
© Royal Tichelaar Makkum

Minale-Maeda • Chroma Key chair + cabinet
Editions of 12 and 3 artist's proofs
Gallery: Droog Design; ToolsGalerie
© Mario Minale

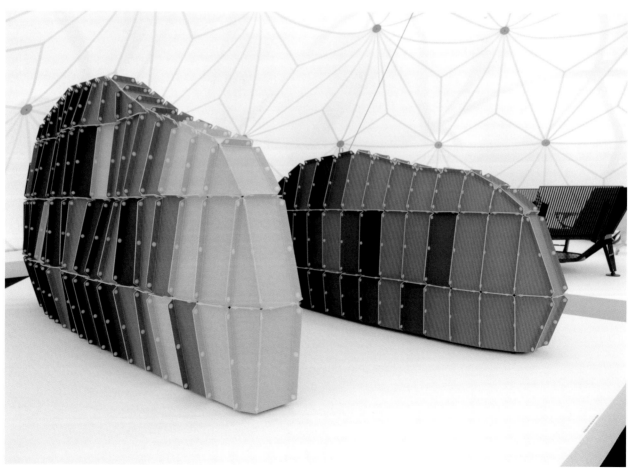

Greg Lynn • The Duke & The Duchess
Edition of 12
Gallery: Vitra
© Vitra
Photo: Thomas Dix

Ronan & Erwan Bouroullec • Rocs
Edition of 12 unique pieces
Gallery: Vitra
© Vitra
Photo: Thomas Dix

Hella Jongerius • Office Pets, Vitra Editions
Edition of 12
Gallery: Vitra
© Hans-Jörg Walter

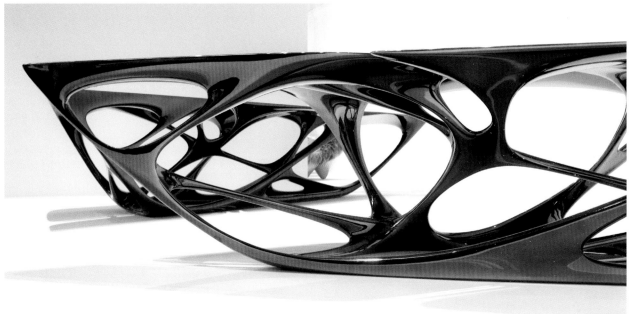

Maarten Baas • Chinese Objects object
Edition of 5
Gallery: Contrasts Gallery
© Contrasts Gallery

Zaha Hadid • Mesa
Edition of 12
Gallery: Vitra
© Vitra
Photo: Eduardo Perez

Rolf Sachs • 3 Equal Parts chair
Edition of 27
© Byron Slater

Rolf Sachs • No Rest for the Rust chair
Edition of 6
© Byron Slater

Ryan Frank · Inkuku
Plastic shopping bags and steel frame
© Stephen Lenthall

Wolfson Design · Line chair
Edition of 10
© Max Nilou

Wolfson Design · Line coffee bench
Edition of 10
© Max Nilou

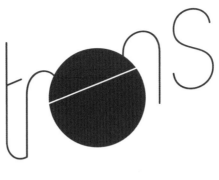

new patrons

Toward the end of the twentieth century, if you took a roll-call of top producer 'names' in design furniture your list would yield mostly Italians — names like Moroso, Cappellini, Flos, Edra, Magis, Alessi, Zanotta — and they would all be manufacturers. But just a few years into the new millennium, we are beginning to see a rather different picture. The most talked-about furniture at the rarefied end of the design market is coming from quite different sources: Friedman Benda, Johnson Trading Gallery and Moss in New York, Contrasts in Shanghai, Kreo and ToolsGalerie in Paris are just some of the new names to drop. These are not industrial producers, but a handful of gallerists, collectors and shop owners. Their products are eye-catching limited editions, collections and one-offs commissioned from a small selection of designers and, occasionally, architects. Although the scale of their output is so tiny that the general public is unlikely even to experience — let alone own — one of these items in real life, images of the pieces and profiles of the designers fill an ever-expanding volume of design-centric media publications reflecting a voyeuristic phenomenon dubbed 'design porn' in some quarters.

There has been a shift in responsibility for encouraging a certain kind of innovation in design. There has also been a shift in public interest about contemporary design objects and a huge shift in the market for them. Manufacturers, it seems, are no longer calling the shots when it comes to experimentation. It is an international design-gallerist elite that are now the new patrons of progress. One of these new patrons, Murray Moss, opened his first shop in New York in 1994 as an 'industrial design store'. When he started, he used to travel around and visit manufacturers at trade fairs such as the Salone del Mobile in Milan or the Ambiente in Frankfurt to order new products directly. At the time, he 'had no direct dialogue, other than social, with the designers', he recalls. Despite outbreaks of independent designer/ producer activity in the 1980s and 1990s, the main way for young designers wanting to get ahead was still to secure a commission from a producer. At the fairs, says Moss, 'I used to meet all these designers dragging around their portfolios and hoping to pitch their ideas to a manufacturer, because of course nothing could ever be realised without making a deal with them — that was how you did it.' So the standard system involved designers tailoring their portfolio projects towards the industrial system, and manufacturers taking the risks by investing in research and bearing the brunt of development and production costs. For a designer, the chances of being commissioned by a manufacturer are small, and for a manufacturer the need for risk minimisation is high.

Moss sensed a high level of frustration among designers around this time. 'This system was not the best system,' he says. It was this frustration, in his view, that helped trigger 'a moment of conversion or confluence', when some designers, restricted by a lack of access to manufacturers, began exploring ideas on their own in their studios with no intention of fully resolving them in a manufacturing sense. 'These ideas would be the equivalent of, let's say, sketches, or first experiments created in a laboratory. They are articulated but not fully resolved, because they don't need to be; their purpose is solely to investigate an idea. They are not like a vacuum cleaner, they don't need to do anything.' Moss was fascinated by this new work and began to keep tabs on it even though it was not yet considered sellable.

Fredrikson Stallard • Pandora chandelier
One-off
Gallery: Swarovski Crystal Palace
© Swarovski Crystal Palace Collection

To be a collector you have to have an eye and conviction.

David Gill

Vincent Dubourg • Napoléon à Trotinette
Edition of 8
Gallery: Carpenters Workshop Gallery
© Carpenters Workshop Gallery

Atelier Van Lieshout • Bad Club Chair
Edition of 20
Gallery: Carpenters Workshop Gallery
© Carpenters Workshop Gallery

Didier Krzentowski, who founded his producer gallery Kreo in 1999, reports having a similar impression to Moss's at the time. 'Until the nineties, designers that were like artists, who need to make extreme pieces, used to go and make them with the Italian furniture companies,' he says, 'but then the market got a bit tougher and [these companies] could not be the research laboratories that they were before... There are a lot of marketing restraints involved in working with big manufacturers. Designers needed to work with more freedom somewhere.' So Krzentowski decided to switch from just collecting art and design to being a producer-gallerist, or patron. He gathered a small stable of innovative designers together, such as Ronan & Erwan Bouroullec, Naoto Fukasawa, Martin Szekely, Hella Jongerius, Pierre Charpin and Jasper Morrison who all shared, in his view, 'zero compromise in the way they work'. He facilitated the production of experimental, limited-edition pieces and collections that he then showed in his gallery space like art objects. Krzentowski says he limited the pieces to editions of around twelve ('like a sculpture or a photograph') because, as an art collector, that was a system he was used to. The designs were often very expensive, time-consuming and difficult to make, so there were financial constraints as well. But although he is at pains to point out that there was no marketing incentive behind limiting the editions of the new pieces, as a collector he was well aware of how much more desirable an object becomes when it is almost unique.

Whereas Krzentowski came from a fine art collector's background, Murray Moss started out in retail, but realised the importance of the art context for these new kinds of 'sketches' quite early on. He took care to locate his shop on Greene Street in the expensive, avant-garde art district of SoHo in New York. 'Presenting work is not neutral,' he says. 'I believe that retailing and the presentation of objects is a very theatrical gesture. It is my job to consider the work and to try to articulate it as clearly and loudly as I can. So I put it in a neighbourhood with a pre-existing defined character, in a particular city, in a certain physical situation, pointedly juxtaposed with other objects or things in a certain room with a certain controlled temperature, with a certain kind of music playing…'

Moss found that because the new design work he was commissioning – from young European designers such as Studio Job, Maarten Baas, Claudy Jongstra and Tord Boontje – was very different in intent from work acquired from manufacturers, there was a need to segregate it from the rest of the interiors products in his shop. He therefore opened a new space next door to his original premises. 'Customers had to leave Moss, the shop, go out into the street and re-enter the space next door which was called "Gallery",' he explains, 'and that physical change is what people needed to understand that there was a different thing going on.' Some time later, Moss knocked a hole in the wall between the two spaces, took the word 'Gallery' out of the window and made the whole thing Moss. 'After three years, people didn't need the road signs, they didn't need to be told that this is "gallery", or "studio" work versus industrial production. They had come to understand that different works, industrial and studio, can benefit from close comparison and in fact speak to each other, illuminate each other and appear more interesting when presented that way. This dual approach to creating work that designers are more and more comfortable with today is what is most exciting about this moment; it is the breakdown of the old "guild" system, and there is no point and nothing to be gained by segregating a designer's industrial design approach from his studio work. In fact, there is much to be learned from seeing them together.'

Jurgen Bey • Pyramids of Makkum
27 individual segments in faïence; silver handles; balsa wood crates; edition of 7
Store: Moss New York / Los Angeles
© Moss

Jurgen Bey • Pyramids of Makkum
Edition of 7
Store: Moss New York / Los Angeles
© Moss

Alexander van Slobbe • Pyramids of Makkum
Edition of 7
Store: Moss New York / Los Angeles
© Moss

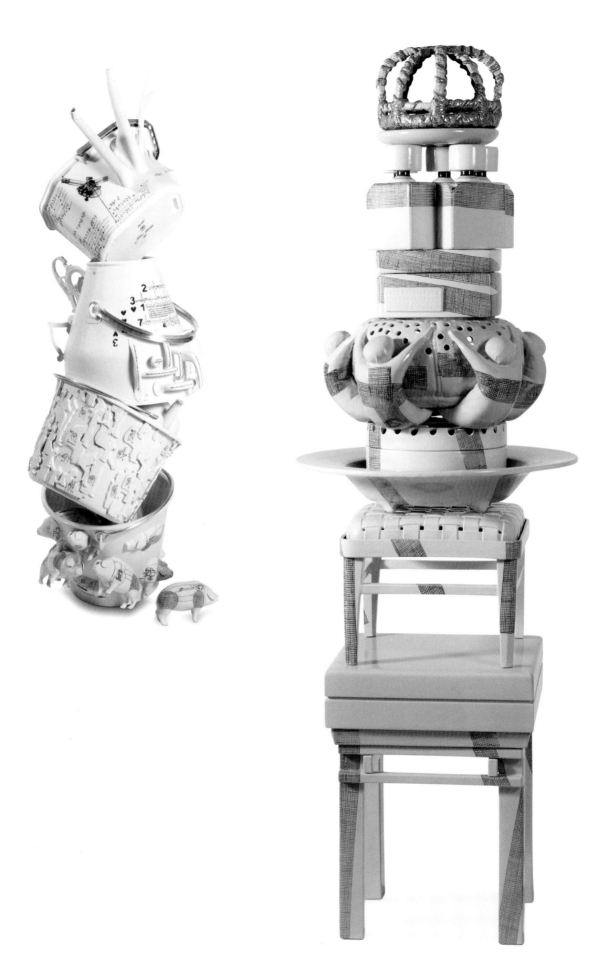

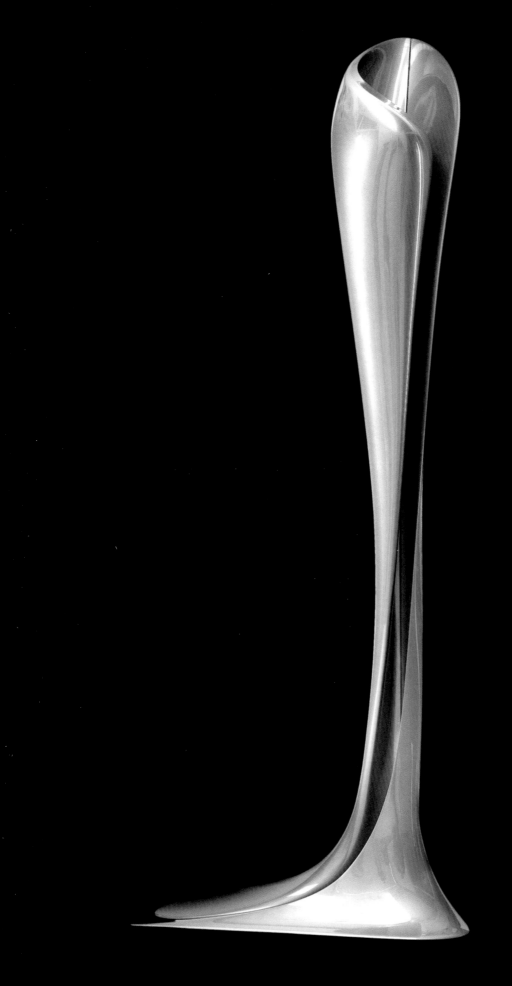

Zaha Hadid • Dune Light
Gallery: David Gill Galleries
© David Gill Galleries
Photo: Slivka Guenzel

Atelier Van Lieshout • Prick Lamp
Edition of 20
Gallery: Carpenters Workshop Gallery
© Carpenters Workshop Gallery

Atelier Van Lieshout • Family Lamp
Edition of 10
Gallery: Carpenters Workshop Gallery
© Carpenters Workshop Gallery

Beyond SoHo, this is an idea that a lot of people are still getting used to. It has become clear that a dual system has developed in design, where designers still continue to create and refine products for manufacturing companies, but are also free to make limited-edition pieces that are shown and sold primarily in galleries. One feature that the limited-edition system has brought with it from the industrial system is an understanding of the need for good branding when establishing a new market. 'The "Design Art" market is at least, if not more, brand driven than the industrialised market,' says Nick Compton, features editor of Wallpaper magazine, who has been following developments in this field for some time. A very short list of key names, such as Newson, Arad, Dixon, Baas, Hadid and Jongerius, represents the top 'labels' and commands the top prices. This is because 'the design art gallerists and dealers are often trying to attract neophyte collectors or art collectors looking to move into design because it is more accessible, both economically and intellectually, than conceptual and contemporary art', Compton explains. 'Brand name designers ease these new collectors into the market and establish instant trust.'

What limited-edition design has appropriated from the art world – apart from its customers – is its system. Not only are the products, or works, exhibited in galleries and dealt on the art market, they are also commissioned in a carefully controlled manner by a growing number of producer-galleries as well. 'We made our first edition objects by Gehry, Pesce, Arad, Kuramata and others more than twenty years ago,' says Rolf Fehlbaum, CEO of the German furniture company Vitra. 'However, at that time there was no market to speak of. The market developed when design in general became collectable for the people who are buying art. That is a phenomenon of the last ten years.' Now that the market is there, production is increasing.

As a manufacturer Vitra is an exception to the rule about design edition producers, but it is unlikely to stay that way for long. It is hard to believe that manufacturers are going to pass up the opportunities for a new market once it shows signs of being established enough, or the media coverage for eye-catching experiments for that matter. But for now, galleries such as Contrasts, Libby Sellers, Carpenters Workshop, Johnson Trading and the Designer's Gallery in Cologne, for example, are leading the way by commissioning editions from established names and/or young unknowns. The production costs involved are very high, and there is a certain degree of pioneering spirit and financial risk involved. Perhaps this is why so many protagonists prefer to talk about experimentation rather than profits. 'For us, editions do not represent a significant business,' says Fehlbaum, 'it is experimentation.' Or: 'I see myself as a patron in a multidisciplinary way,' says Pearl Lam, owner of Contrasts gallery. 'I don't always think about budgets; I just love design.' And Didier Krzentowski of Kreo: 'The gallery is a kind of research laboratory.'

Krzentowski calls his stable of around ten designers a 'family' and talks to them all almost daily on the phone. He says he never really knows how many pieces are going to be made each year, because when his designers do something it is 'to advance design theoretically or practically', not to make pieces for the market: 'I'm not interested in that at all.' Another American gallerist, Paul Johnson, also reveals a drive to push boundaries and even make history: 'An atmosphere of experimentation is the best way to describe what we are doing.' The work produced by his network of young designers is 'not tailored to the market', he says. 'Some people will like it and some will hate it. We are always open to working on projects that have not been done before and have a strong intrinsic value in the historical contexts of design.'

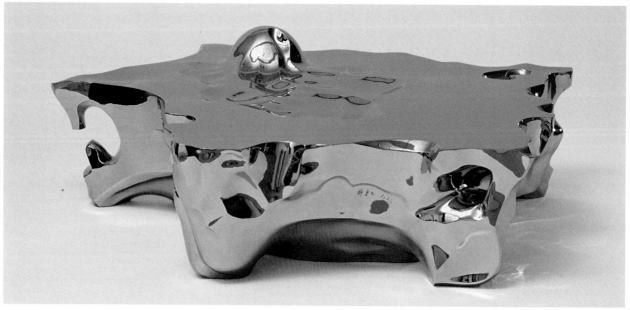

Xavier Lust • Blob IV
Edition of 18
Gallery: Carpenters Workshop Gallery
© Carpenters Workshop Gallery

Shi Jianmin • Coffee table / stool
Edition of 8 plus 2 artist's proofs
Gallery: Gabrielle Ammann // Designer's Gallery
© Gabrielle Ammann // Designer's Gallery

Zaha Hadid • Belu
Edition of 12
Gallery: Kenny Schachter ROVE Projects
© Kenny Schachter ROVE Projects

It is clear that these gallerists understand themselves to be operating very much in the role of patrons in the classical sense, actively devoting themselves to furthering the development of design – like traditional art patrons before them. They choose carefully and work closely with their designers, but how they work together depends upon the dynamic of the individual relationship, says Moss. 'It sometimes happens that I'll sit on the floor of a hotel room with somebody for three days and we'll just talk about ideas. In the case of working with Maarten Baas, I'd say we have a very strong dialogue.' (For example: Moss funded and selected the range of classic furniture items burned by Baas in his debut Smoke series.) 'In the case of Studio Job it's more like a long conversation, followed by another long conversation, and then maybe a year goes by and we meet for breakfast somewhere and they present a fully realised set of drawings – no dialogue encouraged.' In some situations, the projects are fully financed by the galleries, who even help with finding and selecting craftsmen and companies to carry out the execution of the pieces; in others, the work is entirely on commission and the artist has the full burden of realising the work, which the gallery then exhibits, promotes and hopefully sells. Because, patrons or not, the bottom line is: this is business – big business.

In addition to the gallerist patrons, there is an interesting new breed of company becoming involved in the design edition scene. Unlike manufacturers, these companies are not necessarily interested in experimenting in the interests of later mass production, or simply furthering the development of design at an intellectual level. For them the editions themselves are products, and if anything, it is the nature of their manufacture that takes priority, alongside a desire to broaden a particular niche in their market or enhance the company's brand identity. One of the first and best known of these is the Austrian lead crystal company Swarovski. Back in 1989, Swarovski commissioned a range of limited-edition crystal objects from the Italian designers Alessandro Mendini, Ettore Sottsass and Stefano Ricci. Since then, the company has continued to commission and exhibit increasingly spectacular design object collections and installations at fairs and events such at the Salone del Mobile, imm Cologne and Art Miami. For example, its sixth Crystal Palace Collection, shown in Milan in 2008, featured works by Front, Studio Job, Fredrikson Stallard, Marcus Tremonto and Tokujin Yoshioka, to name but a few. Swarovski's proclaimed aim with these attention-grabbing pieces is to 'push the boundaries of crystal and create contemporary interpretations of lighting, furniture and design' – and the editions are certainly spectacular. By combining a well-advised choice of designers with inspired marketing, the company has managed to transform its image with the whole limited-edition phenomenon: even Moss stocks Swarovski.

I see myself as a patron in a multidisciplinary way. I don't always think about the budgets; I just love design.

Pearl Lam

Another company that understands the value of mixing just the right amount of high-profile, innovative designers and architects – such as Zaha Hadid, Jasper Morrison or Amanda Levete – with a meticulously planned branding agenda is Established & Sons. This furniture design and manufacturing company was launched in 2004 by Alasdhair Willis, former publisher of Wallpaper magazine, and Angad Paul, CEO of the Caparo Group, a steel parts manufacturer, with the ambitious aim of revitalising languishing skill sectors from the British automotive industry by producing highly crafted furniture designed by (initially British) designers. Although they also produce 'volume production' furniture objects, Established & Sons was quick to develop and hype their limited-edition ranges with small numbers of highly-priced pieces specifically aimed at the auction or museum market. The company understands the commercial potential of this emerging new design language well, and knows that image is everything. 'The launch of the brand and the press we have chosen to work with have been specifically targeted,' said Willis in a recent interview with hiddenartlondon.co.uk. 'There has been no wastage; it has all been very focused' – leading to a company with a 'very concise and clear message'.

Established & Sons are an interesting blend of manufacturer, branding agency and gallery with a particularly British touch. Parallel to the luxurious elegance of the Around the Corner spatial explorations by Amanda Levete, and Hadid's Aqua tables, they also produce conceptual and provocative pieces such as Jasper Morrison's somewhat Duchampian Crate: an apparently simple wooden box based on a wine crate that created a storm of critical discussion – of the sort usually reserved for art – when it was first shown. In 2007 the company presented a 'non-selling' exhibition where they showed their actual 'volume production' collection remade as one-offs in Carrara marble and mounted on six-metre-high white plinths. The entire purpose of the show was to provoke debate over the 'Design Art' issue by 'reappointing functional designs, iconic in their utility, as opulent objects'. Provoking debate generates discourse, and if everybody is talking about you, you tend to sell more products.

Established & Sons
"4" exhibition overview, Milan 2008
© Mike Golderwater

Zaha Hadid • Swarm chandelier / Aqua table
Company: Established & Sons
© Roland Halbe

Part of the revenue from the sale of Established & Sons' limited-edition pieces at auction and elsewhere gets ploughed back into further research for other products. It is quite an interesting contrast in attitude to that of Didier Krzetowski, but both ultimately achieve the same result because there is a market out there, interested in what they are doing, that they both helped to generate.

Yet another variant of the new edition producers is a company called Meta. Launched in 2008 at the Salone del Mobile by the British antique dealer Mallett, its aim is to 'combine the best of eighteenth-century techniques and materials with twenty-first-century design'. Mallett took on Louise-Anne Comeau and Geoffrey Monge of Atelier Idée (whose clients include Swarovski, Design Miami/Basel, ECAL and LVMH) as creative directors to select a group of designers that included Barber Osgerby, Matali Crasset and Tord Boontje, and then invited them to a workshop to be inspired by the range of skills, tools and materials available to the eighteenth-century decorative arts. Mallett has unparalleled access to an international collection of some of the best specialist antiques restorers in the world. The idea was to turn the skills of these craftspeople back toward production, and revive the tradition of fine furniture using only traditional and precious materials, but with a contemporary language of form. The resulting pieces are surprisingly varied: Ivo 03 (see page 205), a low table by Asymptote made of etched, slumped glass and a rediscovered type of Russian steel from 1780, has an unmistakably computer-generated form, yet Tord Boontje's L'Armoire (see pages 208–9), a veneer cabinet made from rare tropical hardwoods, complete with hidden drawers and secret locks, is so mutant organic, it looks like Art Nouveau on acid.

By targeting this particular niche, Mallett is not only cleverly capitalising on its contacts with over two hundred and fifty master craftspeople worldwide and its client base of decorative art collectors, but also making a strong bid for a return to process and craft in design by deliberately choosing pre-industrial materials and techniques. 'We wanted to have a connection between the eighteenth century and the modern,' says Giles Hutchinson-Smith, managing director of both Mallett and Meta, 'and that link is, of course, the workshop'. The pieces in the collection are limited by the nature of their production process and by the rarity of the materials, rather than by design, says Hutchinson-Smith. 'We make as many as we can, but that's not many. We are even more limited by the obscurity of the material and the difficulty of making the object and the moulds. For example, we only have enough rippled ash and five-thousand-year-old bog oak to make three Wales & Wales desks, and only made enough ingots of Paktong [a nearly extinct seventeenth-century Chinese metal alloy with a gold and silver patina that never tarnishes] to make around twenty-five of Matali Crasset's lanterns.' The value of the Meta products is based in the quality of the craftsmanship and the value of the materials, as well as the individuality of the pieces and the names of their designers.

Debate is essential to a thriving art market — no one talks about it, no one buys anything.

Giles Hutchinson-Smith

These new companies following in the wake of producer-galleries signify the establishment of a growing parallel market for design. The rise in popularity of the trade fair amongst non-industry punters (in 2008, for example, the Salone del Mobile alone had a record-breaking 348,000 visitors, up twenty-nine percent from the previous year) indicates a huge increase in a more design-literate and design-aware public looking for innovation and spectacle. The cross-over of interest in buyers from the art world also points to design being an accessible alternative to art, capable of furnishing an equally rich palette of content, narrative and historical context. 'Design is a young discipline,' says Rolf Fehlbaum. 'It has many aspects and is still developing. Some designers have great skills in working conceptually and are maybe more interested in concept than product. Editions are a very good way for them to make unusual objects and get paid for it. Their clients are people who have an art approach to design. I think it is great that this market exists. On the other hand, normal design, democratic design, is alive and well. It is just a completely different world.'

Studio Makkink & Bey • Exhibition Overview
Gallery: Contrasts Gallery at Design Miami/Basel, June 2008
© Contrasts Gallery
Photo: James Harris

Studio Makkink & Bey • Cleaning-Beauty-Bed
Gallery: Contrasts Gallery at Design Miami/Basel, June 2008
© Contrasts Gallery
Photo: James Harris

Studio Makkink & Bey • Cleaning-Beauty-Dustpan
Gallery: Contrasts Gallery at Design Miami/Basel, June 2008
© Contrasts Gallery
Photo: James Harris

Fernando and Humberto Campana • Cartoon chair
Gallery: Albion
© Fernando and Humberto Campana and Albion
Photo: Ed Reeve

Fernando and Humberto Campana • Transplastic chairs
Prototypes
Gallery: Albion
© Fernando and Humberto Campana and Albion
Photo: Ed Reeve

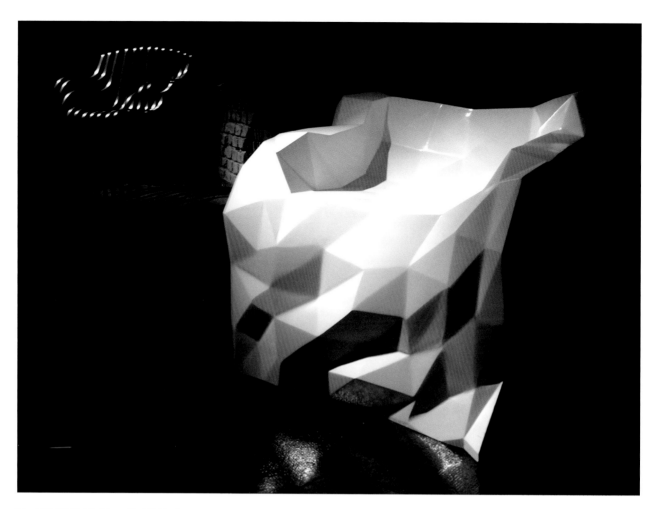

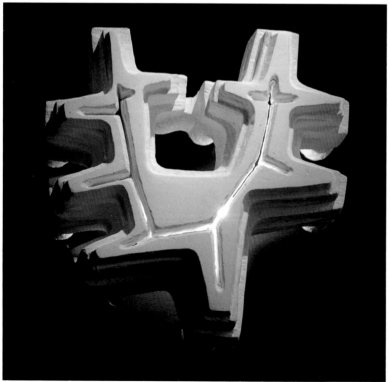

Julian Mayor • General Dynamic
Edition of 10
Gallery: FAT Galerie
© Severine Van Wersch

Terence Main • Pair of plaster wall sconces
© Magen H Gallery

Galerie Downtown François Laffanour
at Design Miami/Basel, June 2008
© Design Miami/Basel
Photo: James Harris

R 20th Century gallery
at Design Miami/Basel, June 2008
© Design Miami/Basel
Photo: James Harris

My job is to respond, to wake up every day and say, 'Okay, the people who I'm interested in are making this work'. If Hella Jongerius decided to make cakes and I was interested in that, then I would have to open up a diner.
Murray Moss

Sebastian Brajkovic • Lathe Chair VIII
Bronze, hand-embroidered; edition of 8
Gallery: Carpenters Workshop Gallery
© Carpenters Workshop Gallery

Sebastian Brajkovic • Lathe Chair V
Bronze, hand-embroidered; edition of 8
Gallery: Carpenters Workshop Gallery
© Carpenters Workshop Gallery

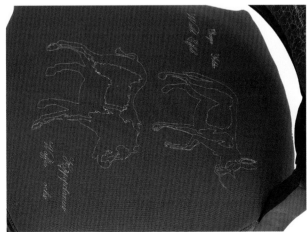

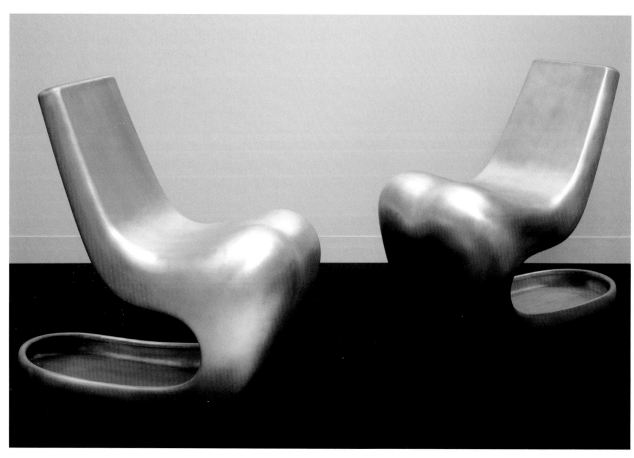

Wendell Castle • Seneca Hall table
Edition of 8
Gallery: Carpenters Workshop Gallery
© Carpenters Workshop Gallery

Satyendra Pakhalé • Alu Rocking Chair
Edition of 7 plus 3 artist's proofs
Gallery: Gabrielle Ammann // Designer's Gallery
© Gabrielle Ammann // Designer's Gallery
Photo: Pirmin Rösli

Wendell Castle • Nirvana
Edition of 8
Gallery: Carpenters Workshop Gallery
© Carpenters Workshop Gallery

Wendell Castle • Abilene rocking chair
Edition of 8
Gallery: Carpenters Workshop Gallery
© Carpenters Workshop Gallery

Wendell Castle • Lucky Day
Edition of 8
Gallery: Carpenters Workshop Gallery
© Carpenters Workshop Gallery

Wendell Castle • Black Widow
Edition of 8
Gallery: Carpenters Workshop Gallery
© Carpenters Workshop Gallery

Wendell Castle • Triad chair
Edition of 8
Gallery: Carpenters Workshop Gallery
© Carpenters Workshop Gallery

Public perception of the market has intensified because the media have been really focusing on it. But it's always been here and it's part of our culture... the patron, the connoisseur, the collector have always been around.

Alexander Payne

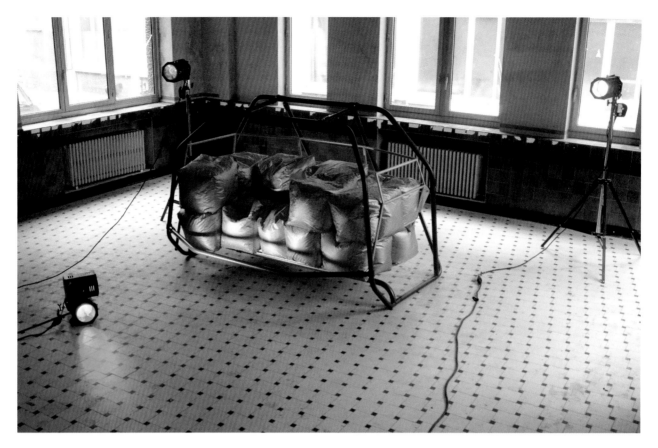

Olivier Peyricot • Copper Shelter sofa
Gallery: ToolsGalerie
© Olivier Peyricot

Johanna Grawunder • Rotondo
Edition of 6, 2 artist's proofs and 2 prototypes
Gallery: Galerie Italienne
© Santi Caleca

Gabrielle Ammann // Designer's Gallery
Emmanuel Babled exhibition, 2006
© Gabrielle Ammann // Designer's Gallery

Gabrielle Ammann // Designer's Gallery
Johanna Grawunder exhibition, 2007
© Gabrielle Ammann // Designer's Gallery

Martino Gamper • Off-Cuts – Total Trattoria project
Gallery: The Aram Gallery
© Nilufar
Photo: Angus Mills

Aranda / Lasch • Quasi Table
Edition of 6
Gallery: Johnson Trading Gallery
© Shira Agmon Hargrave

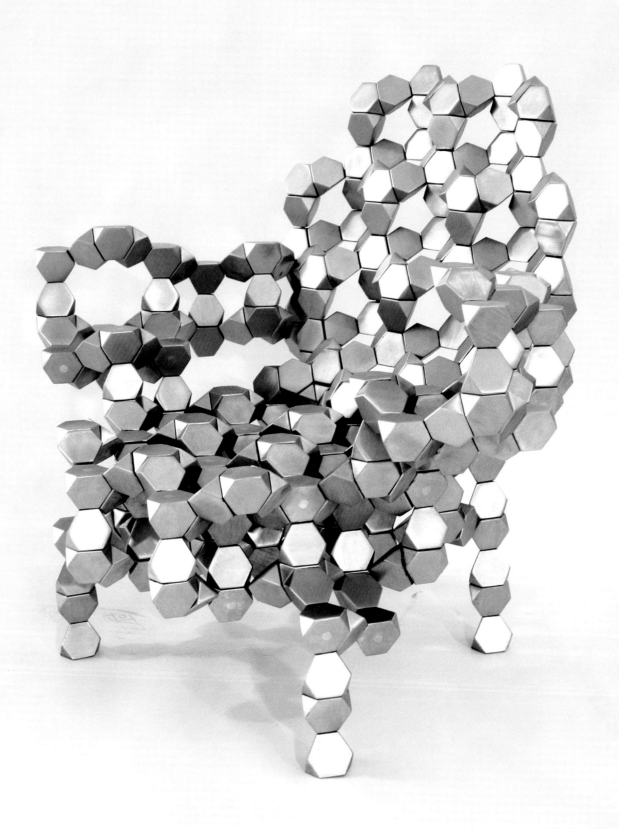

Aranda / Lasch • Fauteuil Chair
Prototype + edition of 6
Gallery: Johnson Trading Gallery
© Shira Agmon Hargrave

Aranda / Lasch • Quasi Cabinet
Edition of 10
Gallery: Johnson Trading Gallery
© Shira Agmon Hargrave

Audiences are looking at these types of works differently, they aren't just pieces of furniture, but artworks that can also be functional.

Pearl Lam

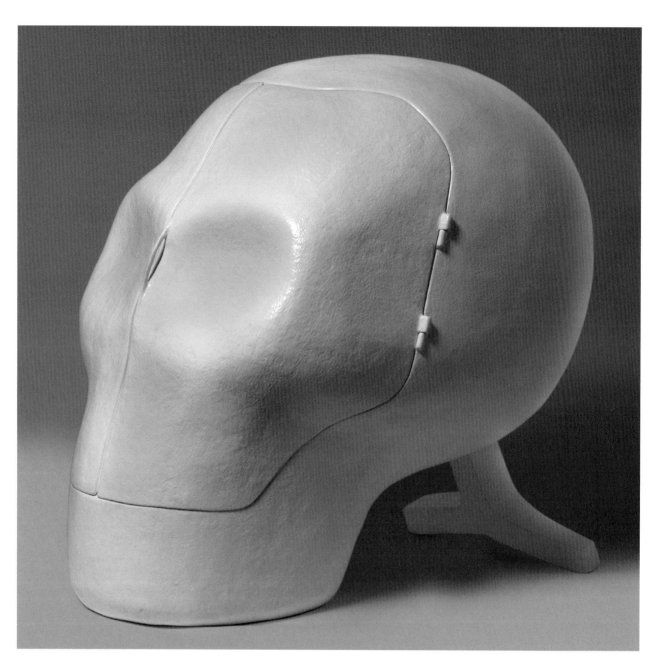

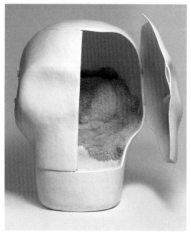

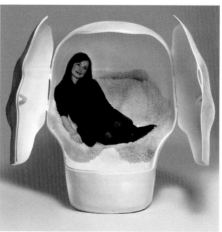

Atelier Van Lieshout · Sensory Deprivation Skull
Edition of 10
Gallery: Carpenters Workshop Gallery
© Carpenters Workshop Gallery

Ronan and Erwan Bouroullec · The Stitch Room
Installation in the 'MyHome' group exhibition at
Vitra Design Museum, 2007
Gallery: Vitra Design Museum
© Ronan and Erwan Bouroullec

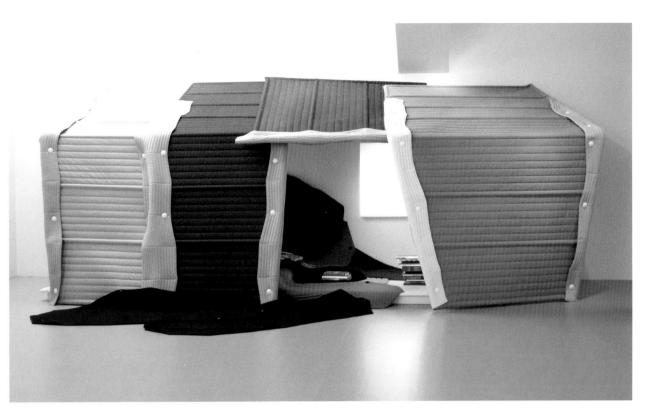

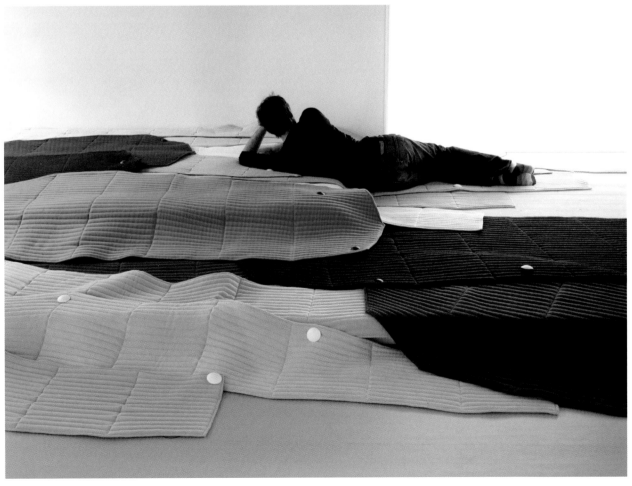

There is a
continual discussion
between ourselves and the
designers and the ateliers
because everyone's reputation is
at stake on this and we don't want
to trip up on something that hasn't
been thought out in the most perfect
way. Attention to detail is
essential: you only get that
through communication
really.

Gilles Hutchinson-Smith

'Stools' show; September, 2007
Gallery: Galerie Kreo
© Galerie Kreo
Photo: Fabrice Gousset

Adrien Rovero • Portique lamp
Gallery: Galerie Kreo
© Galerie Kreo
Photo: Fabrice Gousset

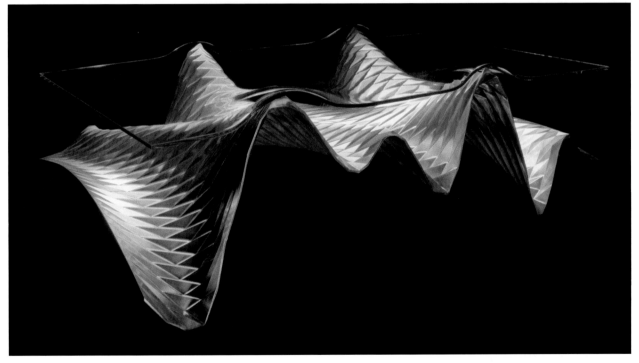

Edward Barber & Jay Osgerby · Cupola
Venini handblown glass, double incalmo, mezza filigrana, cast
and spun mirror-polished white bronze, Carrara marble base
Client: Meta
© Meta

Wales & Wales · Glissade
Ash (desk), olive ash (legs), boxwood (hinges), chestnut (dust
board), red lacquer (pen box), custom dyed leather (hidden well),
hand-crafted wooden wheels and hinges
Client: Meta
© Meta

Asymptote (Hani Rashid & Lise Anne Couture) · Ivo
Rare Tula steel and slumped glass, hand-etched and polished
Client: Meta
© Meta

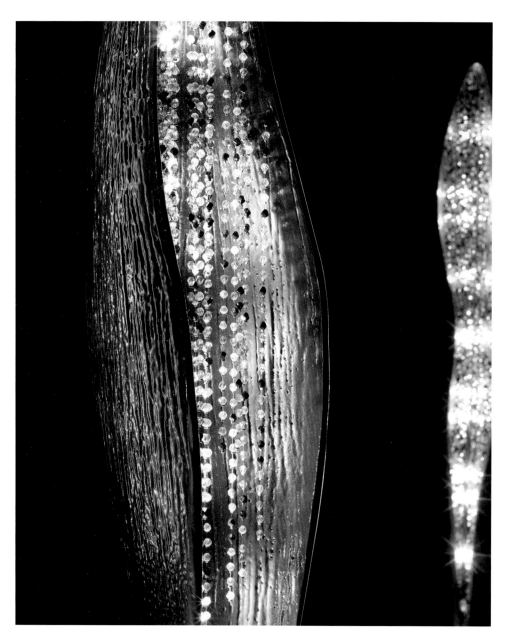

Arne Quinze · Ellipsis (details)
Gallery: Swarovski Crystal Palace at
Salone del Mobile, Milan 2008
© Swarovski Crystal Palace Collection

Marcel Wanders · Shower Chandeliers
Gallery: Swarovski Crystal Palace at
Salone del Mobile, Milan 2008
© Swarovski Crystal Palace Collection

Tord Boontje • L'Armoire
Traditionally sawn cocobolo over mahogany and okoumé
structure, hidden compartments, secret locking mechanisms
Client: Meta
© Meta

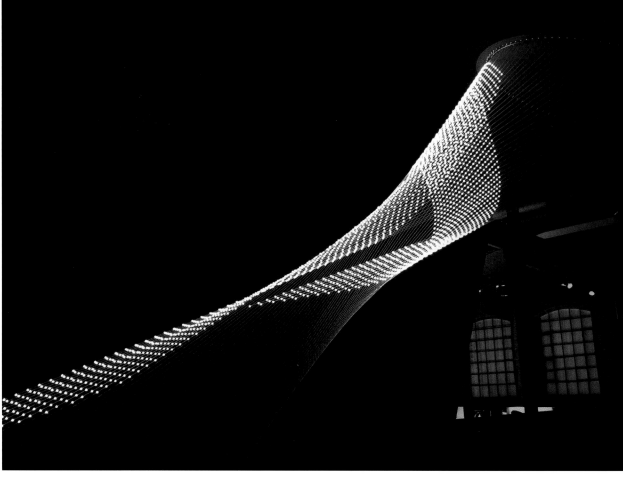

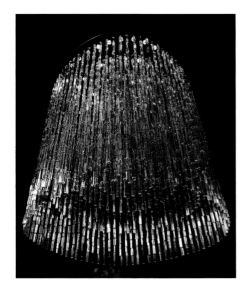

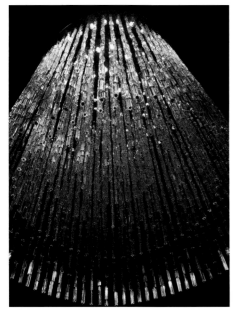

Exhibition overview
Gallery: Swarovski Crystal Palace at Salone del Mobile,
Milan 2008
© Swarovski Crystal Palace Collection

Zaha Hadid · Ré
Gallery: Swarovski Crystal Palace at Salone del Mobile,
Milan 2008
© Swarovski Crystal Palace Collection

Pierro Lissoni · Cupola (details)
Gallery: Swarovski Crystal Palace at Salone del Mobile,
Milan 2008
© Swarovski Crystal Palace Collection

Pierro Lissoni · Cupola
Gallery: Swarovski Crystal Palace at Salone del Mobile,
Milan 2008
© Swarovski Crystal Palace Collection

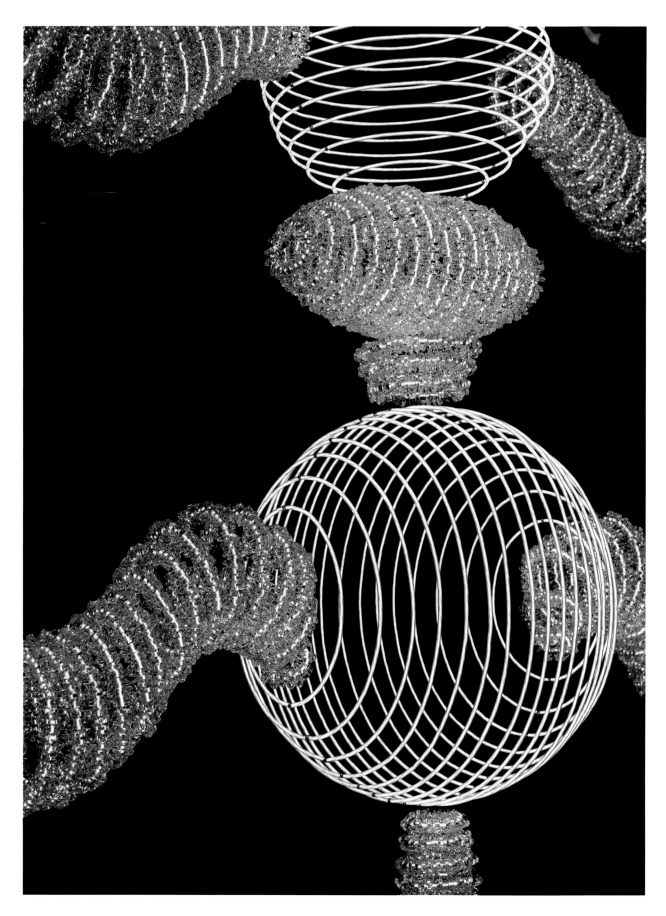

Marcus Tremonto • Double Solo (detail)
Crystals and electro-luminescent wire
Gallery: Swarovski Crystal Palace at Salone del Mobile,
Milan 2008
© Swarovski Crystal Palace Collection

Tokujin Yoshioka • Eternal
Giant chaton-cut crystals embedded in acrylic; edition of 41
Gallery: Swarovski Crystal Palace at Salone del Mobile,
Milan 2008
© Swarovski Crystal Palace Collection

Tokujin Yoshioka • Eternal
In production
© Swarovski Crystal Palace Collection

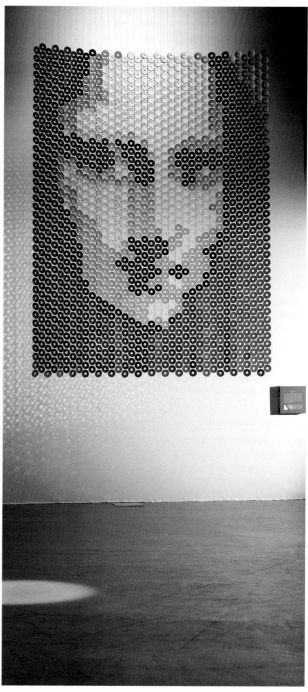

Paul Cocksedge · Veil
Four-metre-high curtain made of 1,440 crystals
Gallery: Swarovski Crystal Palace at Salone del Mobile,
Milan 2008
© Swarovski Crystal Palace Collection

Xavier Lust · Archiduchaise
Gallery: Carpenters Workshop Gallery
© Carpenters Workshop Gallery

The gallerist is held accountable in the end for the type of work produced and sold to their clients. Therefore I feel that they need to be involved in all areas of production. As an advisor and expert you can determine flaws that customers might not notice.

Paul Johnson

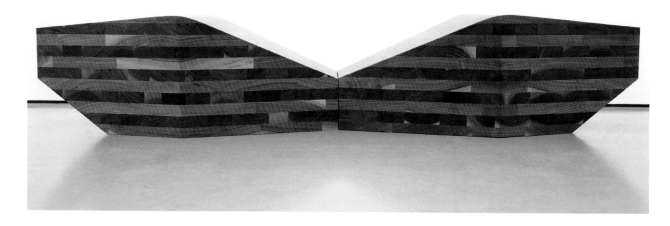

David Adjaye • Monoforms
Gallery: Albion
© David Adjaye and Albion
Photo: Ed Reeve

Peter Marigold • Split Boxes
Gallery: Gallery Libby Sellers
© Gallery Libby Sellers

Maria Pergay • Solo exhibition 2007
Gallery: Jousse Entreprise
© Jousse Entreprise
Photo: Marc Domage

Maria Pergay • Conference table
Gallery: Jousse Entreprise
© Adrien Dirand

Arik Levy • Fractal Cloud
Kenny Schachter ROVE Projects at Design Miami/Basel,
December 2007
© Design Miami/Basel
Photo: Andy Keate

'Design A–Z' exhibition, 2007
Exhibition view
Gallery: mitterand + cramer
© Claude Cortinovis

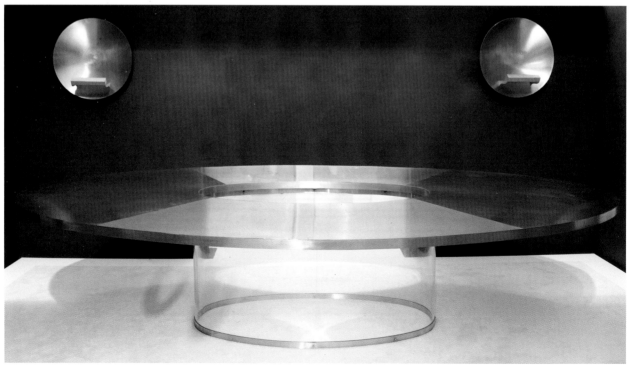

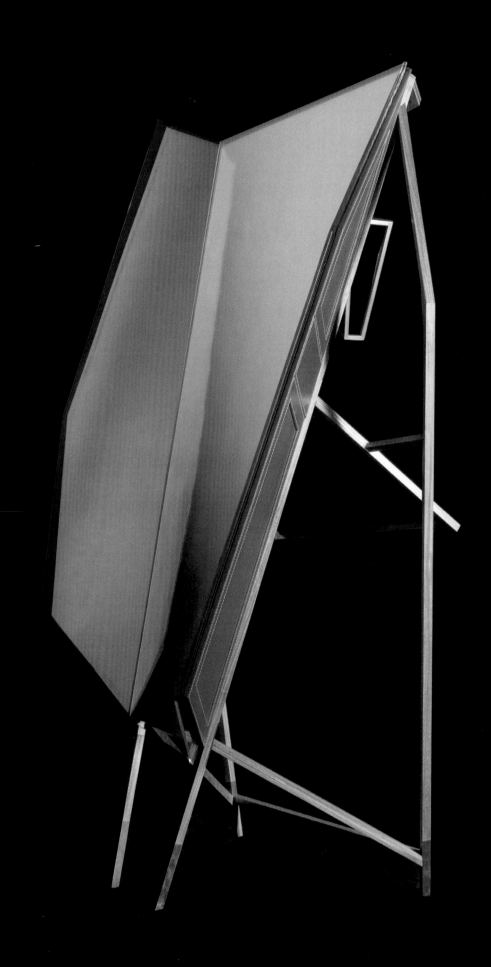

Matali Crasset • Diamonds Are a Girl's Best Friend 1
Paktong cast using lost wax method, unique repeating master-
link chain, handblown sheet glass
Client: Meta
© Meta

**Established & Sons • Drift Bench by Amanda Levete and Writing
Desk by Michael Young**
'Elevating Design' exhibition view at London Design Festival 2007
Designs from the 'volume production' collection remade as one-
offs in Carrara marble
Company: Established & Sons
© Mark C. O'Flaherty

There are more possibilities now and that is good for us all. It makes the world of design bigger and stronger. That's a good thing!
Job Smeets

Studio Job · Globe
Edition of 3 plus 1 artist's proof
Gallery: Swarovski Crystal Palace at Salone del Mobile,
Milan 2008
© Swarovski Crystal Palace Collection

Ron Arad · MT Rocker
Gallery: Friedman Benda
© Friedman Benda, New York

Roger Tallon · Bridge Armchair, module 400
Gallery: Jousse Entreprise
© 2008, ProLitteris, Zurich

auct

Led by Sotheby's and Phillips de Pury & Company, international auction houses began holding dedicated design object sales in the late 1990s and have played a key role in shaping the new Limited Edition / Design Art market. They initially concentrated on vintage twentieth-century furniture pieces together with a handful of prototypes, editions and one-offs from the – now familiar – ranks of established designers such as Ron Arad, Ross Lovegrove, Marc Newson and the architect Zaha Hadid. But as the vintage pieces got rarer and more expensive, and interest in experimental contemporary pieces remained keen, the number of contemporary design works being put up for sale began to increase. Riskier works also started to appear from younger designers, some of them fresh from college and with hardly any track record, causing ripples of disapproval from the more conservative corners of the market.

There are signs of big changes afoot in the most traditional, establishment and cliquey world of the auction room. Not only is design now being dealt like art and – far more interestingly – being bought by art collectors, but auction houses are beginning to open up and become more user-friendly, which is attracting a whole new generation of cash-rich collectors with contemporary tastes. The pieces that some of these designers have been producing for years have not altered much, says designer Tom Dixon. 'What's changed is that the art market has become interested.' The art market has been bullish for a while and prices are accordingly astronomical, but there is also a feeling of saturation and a sense that the new millennium's creative zeitgeist is not adequately expressed by fine art alone. 'Designers are taking more risks, they can be more conceptual and think more artistically,' says Shanghai-based gallerist Pearl Lam, who deals in both contemporary fine art and design. 'Audiences are looking at these types of work differently. They aren't just pieces of furniture, but artworks that can also be functional.'

Collecting contemporary or limited-edition design is still in its infancy and is not as restricted by traditional boundaries and exclusive territories as the established art market. This means that it is more accessible to buyers, and there is more room for innovation in terms of how and why pieces are traded as well as commissioned. 'The collectors for design are changing,' says Richard Wright, founder of the Wright auction house in Chicago. 'The influx of art collectors actively buying is an important shift, both in their willingness to spend but also in what that signifies: design as the expression of the collector, not just quiet furniture that recedes into the room.' Giles Hutchinson-Smith, a director of the British fine antique furniture firm Mallet and its new contemporary design offshoot Meta, agrees, and adds that design collecting has a lot to do with personal branding. 'Collectors love the idea of being able to mix contemporary with traditional because it has an amazingly chic look about it. Not only does it look like they are educated and cultured in the past, but educated and cultured in the future as well, and that's a really important message... All collecting, from the ancient Greeks to the twenty-first century, is about the image of the collectors and what people think about them.'

Shigeru Ban • PTH-02 Paper Tea House
Gallery: Phillips de Pury & Company, London
© Phillips de Pury & Company

With so many multimillionaires around that there are even dedicated trade shows catering to their liquid assets, standard luxury status symbols such as cars, yachts and handbags have become almost commonplace. It is now far more fashionable to add polish to the personal identity with a house (or houses) furnished in a collection of contemporary one-offs and limited-edition pieces to match the art and the architecture. 'Some of these collectors are not educated in the history of design or simply not interested,' says Wright. 'There is always a drive to do something new.' Buying design is no longer just for an insider clique of informed establishment enthusiasts, but for anyone who can afford it. This may also explain why contemporary design objects being sold at auction are increasingly presented in a retail context rather than the traditional historical or collector's format. When Richard Wright founded his auction house together with his wife in 2000, they revolutionised the industry by publishing beautifully designed, magazine-style glossy catalogues for their sales, packed with well-shot colour images of the individual lots. It brought the buying experience closer to the shopping experience and, in so doing, paved the way for a more user-friendly type of auction.

I think what we're talking about is a subject that's broken boundaries.

That's not a bubble that's going to burst, that's evolution... Finally, the medieval guilds system has been crushed and people are free, as they are in art, to move where they wish.

Murray Moss

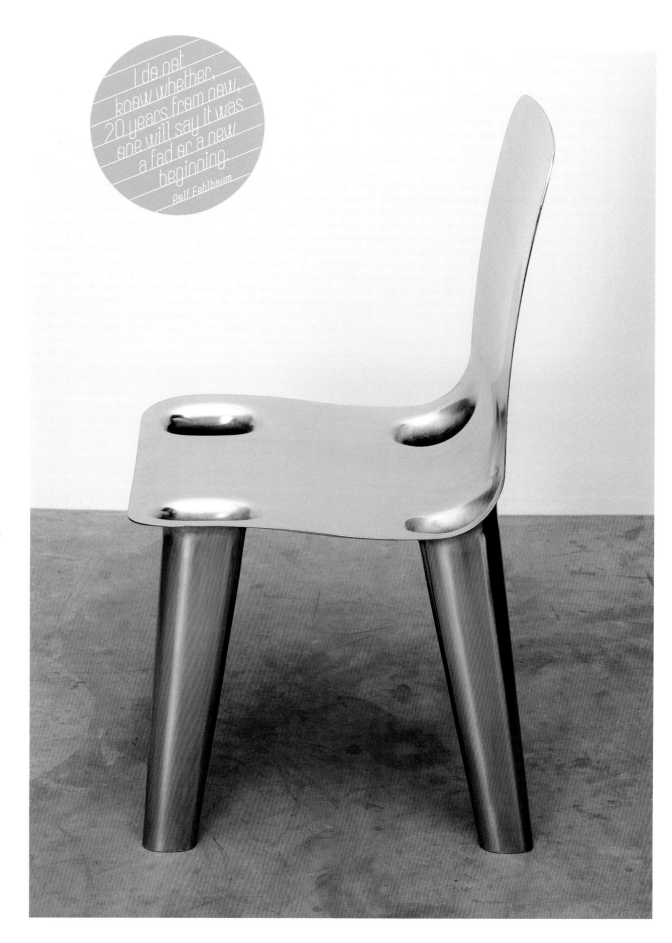

I do not
know whether,
20 years from now,
one will say it was
a fad or a new
beginning.

Rolf Fehlbaum

Marc Newson • Nickel chair
Edition of 10
Gallery: Gagosian Gallery
© Marc Newson; Gagosian Gallery

Marc Newson • Carbon Fibre chair
Edition of 250
Gallery: Gagosian Gallery
© Marc Newson; Gagosian Gallery

Marc Newson • Black Hole table
Carbon fibre
Gallery: Phillips de Pury & Company, New York
© Phillips de Pury & Company

Phillips de Pury & Company have adopted a similar approach to Wright, and have online catalogues packed with attractive images as well as clear instructions as to how the auction process works. They have also taken the preview experience out of the obscure storeroom-like atmosphere and into an airy modern space with their new building at Howick Place in London. Here they host selling exhibitions too, of works from designers including Hani Rashid, Marcus Tremonto, Rolf Sachs and Vitra. The atmosphere here is more that of a contemporary gallery or a smart concept store than an old English auction establishment. 'I don't see ourselves as just a house for moving product and objects along through the market place,' says Phillips' Design Director Alexander Payne. 'I see us as proactively looking; creating and curating auctions that are stimulating and showing the best of the best in cutting edge contemporary design culture. That means going out and searching for the right pieces that make sense, and not just sitting back and waiting for them to come in.' Following the traditional formula of simply cataloguing and selling goods and chattels is no longer appropriate for today's market, culture and clients, Payne believes. 'We have to create and present works in a way that stimulates and engages the collector's mind.'

So the clear-cut divisions between auction houses and galleries are starting to fade. The tradition of galleries having (often exclusive) agreements with artists and being the primary sales outlet for their works, whilst the high-end auction houses concerned themselves with the secondary market (representing owners' consignments and reselling pieces from collections or stock) is no longer the rule. Auction houses are now to be found collaborating with galleries on selling exhibitions and even, in some cases, bypassing the gallery altogether and selling works by artists and designers directly. 'Auctions are transactional, galleries are relational,' says Richard Wright. 'The primary market is best served by galleries, the secondary market by auctions, but auctions are bridging that gap and acting as galleries.' Wright says this is an appropriate strategy when working with material that does not have an established value: such as the young limited-edition market.

Hani Rashid • LQ Chandelier de Pury and Baldaquin de Pury
Edition of 5 and edition of 5 plus 3 prototypes respectively
Gallery: 'Atmospherics' exhibition; Phillips de Pury & Company, New York
© Phillips de Pury & Company

Fernando and Humberto Campana • Prived Oca chandelier from the Crystal Palace Collection
Unique; raffia and Swarovski crystals
Gallery: Phillips de Pury & Company, New York
© Phillips de Pury & Company

There seem to be two key reasons for this remixing of roles in relation to the design market. The first is the excitement surrounding limited-edition design, which has created a Klondike-style atmosphere as buyers and sellers alike seek to cash in on the steep price rises. The second is that designers often have a totally different kind of relationship with galleries than artists do. Designers do not tend to have exclusive relationships with any of their clients, because of the broad range of fields in which they work. For example, they may have mass-production contracts for a set of cutlery with one manufacturer, a coffee table range with another, design a site-specific hotel interior or a house for a private client, and then do a limited-edition collection for an exhibition with a gallery. Designers tend to be self-employed entities who are not (yet) embedded in the network of agents and system regulations that can both protect and hamper at the same time. 'That's the way designers work,' says Sotheby's Director of Twentieth Century Design, James Zemaitis. 'They are much more willing to think outside the box when it comes to marketing themselves, whereas I think your typical contemporary artist signs up with the first gallerist that shows a serious interest in him or her, and then later chooses the gallery that is going to give the best deal. Whatever gallery they are with, it's much more exclusive. In my experience you will not see today's contemporary art stars – with the exception of Damien Hirst – working directly with an auction house.'

Mathias Bengtsson • Slice chairs
Early prototypes in aluminium and wood
Gallery: Phillips de Pury & Company, New York
© Phillips de Pury & Company

For the designers, the advantages of their work being handled and looked at in an art context are clear, says Tom Dixon. 'Museums and galleries are much better for explaining ideas... You have a catalogue, you have a lot of white space around the object, and can explain the process and the conceptual underpinning of the piece in a way that you just can't in a design shop or a retail shop or a trade fair. So there's space to talk about ideas, which is great.'

The more design is talked about in this context, the more valuable it seems to become. Marc Newson's 1985 limited-edition (ten pieces) Lockheed Lounge is now considered to be one of the key, iconic design objects of its time that has transcended the realms of functional furniture entirely. One example was sold by Christie's in 2000 for $105,000. Just six years later, the prototype sold for almost $1 million at auction with Sotheby's and was later sold again privately for an estimated $2.5 million. Yet another Lockheed Lounge went for $1.5 million at Christie's again in 2007. Prices like these – and there are similar examples for pieces from the likes of Arad, Hadid, Dixon and Co. – do not just indicate that the market is hot: they show that contemporary society now considers great design to be just as valid, significant and important as great art, which is an interesting development. The designer Marcus Tremonto, who also works as a consultant for Phillips de Pury & Company, points out that, although there is a handful of designers consistently making headlines with top prices, there are other less-publicised sales that are just as telling. 'The interest is there, it unfortunately doesn't make for as much newsworthy dialogue when we sell something from Dunne & Raby for £20,000 or £10,000, for example.' Dunne & Raby are two British designers making highly conceptual design objects, which are arguably at the more difficult end of the market, but their soft-toy format Huggable Atomic Mushrooms are selling well for around £2,000 a piece, says Tremonto.

Names matter because the names are there for a reason.

Ron Arad, Marc Newson, Zaha Hadid are not just a marketing phenomenon, they are the best of their time.

That said, I would rather have the best work of a lesser-known designer than a mediocre example from a top-tier name. Quality is the goal.

Richard Wright

Wolfson Design • Gold box
© Wolfson Design

Wolfson Design • Gold box
© Wolfson Design

Wolfson Design • Genoa desk
Edition of 10
Gallery: Patrick Brillet Fine Art
© Maxim Nilov

We watch and nurture.
Alexander Payne

Nevertheless, the gold-rush atmosphere in the market does – and will continue to – produce casualties. The 'anything goes' attitude makes for innovation and interesting developments, but can also cause instability. Also, because the secondary market for contemporary design has yet to be properly defined, there is a big risk of judgement error all round. 'I think that the design market is in for some bumps,' says James Zemaitis. 'There's way too much product out there, there are way too many experiments that go awry on the auction market, and there's too much pressure for materials to be developed, so tons of mistakes are made.' Our image-based society with its accelerated attention span is also prone to attention-deficit problems and can all too easily mistake novelty for quality. There is a lot of work on the market from designers with no proven track record in this field. Nevertheless, Zemaitis believes that the interest in contemporary design is here to stay – and for good reason. 'I think that there is enough depth, enough great things happening, that even if the economy forces a slowdown in the market, coupled with bad decisions being made by auction houses with a heavy glut of material, the long term is going to be very, very healthy.'

In a 2008 New York Times article, the design critic Alice Rawsthorn stated that 'design art is a commercial phenomenon, not a cultural one'. In some respects she is absolutely right, if you consider the term to be a fashion label or branding vehicle. But that would be ignoring the very real role that contemporary design of this kind is fulfilling. If the role of artists is to reflect their society and its issues and help bring new insights into the nature of that society, one would have to say that design is in some ways sharing that role for our era. 'Limited-edition furniture is about personalisation, and speaks to the collector's and the individual's need for uniqueness,' says Marcus Tremonto. We have too many choices, and many of them are the wrong kind of choice. Every day we are being tricked into feeling that the products we live with are individually programmed to fit our unique needs, when we know full well that millions of others own exactly the same products and have exactly the same range of choices. 'What was once defined by its mission and purpose at production, its form and function, is being redefined because of the way it is consumed and collected,' says journalist Nick Compton. Design is undergoing a renaissance: it now has to fill new roles that bring aesthetic content, narrative and a sense of identity to the jaded consumer, as well as providing opportunities for alternative expression and experimentation for the designer. This is a mandate that goes way beyond markets and price tags. Perhaps in twenty or thirty years we will be able to look back and decide whether the whole thing was just a delayed, decadent, fin-de-siècle outburst, or the beginning of a new era.

It's not just about a market, this design is visionary and laboratory driven, that for me is very exciting.
James Zemaitis

Marc Newson • Micarta chair
Linen phenolic composite; edition of 10
Gallery: Gagosian Gallery
© Marc Newson; Gagosian Gallery

Marc Newson • Solo exhibition, 2008
Limited-edition collection in white Carrara marble
Gallery: Gagosian Gallery
© Gagosian Gallery

Marc Newson • Voronoi shelf
White Carrara marble; edition of 8
Gallery: Gagosian Gallery
© Marc Newson; Gagosian Gallery

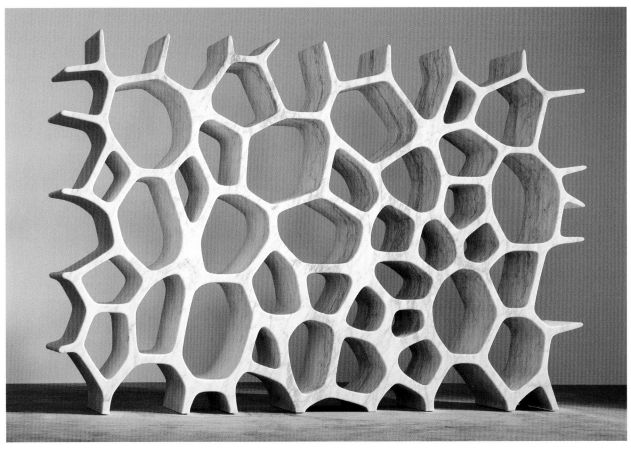

Rolf Sachs • Leaden
Pair of blackened cast lead chairs; edition of 7
Gallery: Phillips de Pury & Company, New York
© Phillips de Pury & Company

Maarten Baas • Where There's Smoke chairs
From an edition of 25
Gallery: Sotheby's 20th Century Design
© Sotheby's 20th Century Design

It takes years for the importance of pieces to be discovered.

So for every immediately hot, immediately whoa piece, like Laarman's Bone Chair or Verhoeven's Cinderella Chair, with immediate recognition and value, you've got to figure that there are a great number of things being made and exhibited, that don't get picked up by the manufacturer or turned into a limited edition.

James Zemaitis

Design Art has not changed the art market; it is the other way around. Gagosian's representation of Marc Newson is a quantum shift in the design world; I don't think it made a big impact in Larry's life.

Richard Wright

Rolf Sachs · Aladdin Lamp (detail)
Borosilicate glass, boxwood stand, neon gas; edition of 7
Gallery: Phillips de Pury & Company, New York
© Phillips de Pury & Company

Stuart Haygarth · Tail Light
Gallery: Gallery Libby Sellers
© Stuart Haygarth

Johanna Grawunder • Protanoplia
Stainless steel, hand-sewn gold mesh, coloured fluorescent
tubes; unique
Gallery: Wright
© Wright
Photo: Brian Franczyk Photography

Johanna Grawunder • Giolight I
Gallery: Phillips de Pury & Company, New York
© Phillips de Pury & Company

I don't see ourselves as just a house for moving products along and objects through the market place.

I see us as proactively looking, creating and curating auctions that are stimulating and showing the best of the best of cutting edge of contemporary design and culture.

That means going out and finding the pieces that make sense and not just sitting back and waiting for them to come in.

Alexander Payne

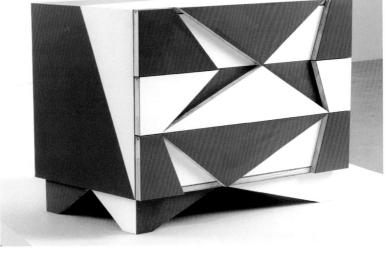

A name operates the same way in the design world as it does in the fashion or film industry. There is association involved, which automatically gives people confidence and assurance. This is why people buy into labels.

Stuart Haygarth

Alessandro Mendini • Scivolando chair
Mirrored glass and wood
Gallery: Phillips de Pury & Company, New York
© Phillips de Pury & Company

Martino Gamper • Unique secretaire cabinet
From the exhibition 'Gio Ponti translated by Martino Gamper'
Assembled from furniture originally designed by Gio Ponti for the
Hotel Parco dei Principi, Sorrento, Italy, 1960
Gallery: Phillips de Pury & Company, New York
© Phillips de Pury & Company

Martino Gamper • Unique chest of drawers
From the exhibition 'Gio Ponti translated by Martino Gamper'
Assembled from furniture originally designed by Gio Ponti for the
Hotel Parco dei Principi, Sorrento, Italy, 1960
Gallery: Phillips de Pury & Company, New York
© Phillips de Pury & Company

Philippe Bestenheider · Alice armchair
Polished aluminium; edition of 15 plus 3 artist's proofs
Gallery: Nilufar
© Wright
Photo: Brian Franczyk Photography

Michael Coffey · Serpent coffee table
One-off
Gallery: Wright
© Wright
Photo: Brian Franczyk Photography

Anthony Dunne and Fiona Raby in collaboration with Michael Anastassiades · Hide Away Furniture, Type 01
Gallery: Phillips de Pury & Company, New York
© Phillips de Pury & Company

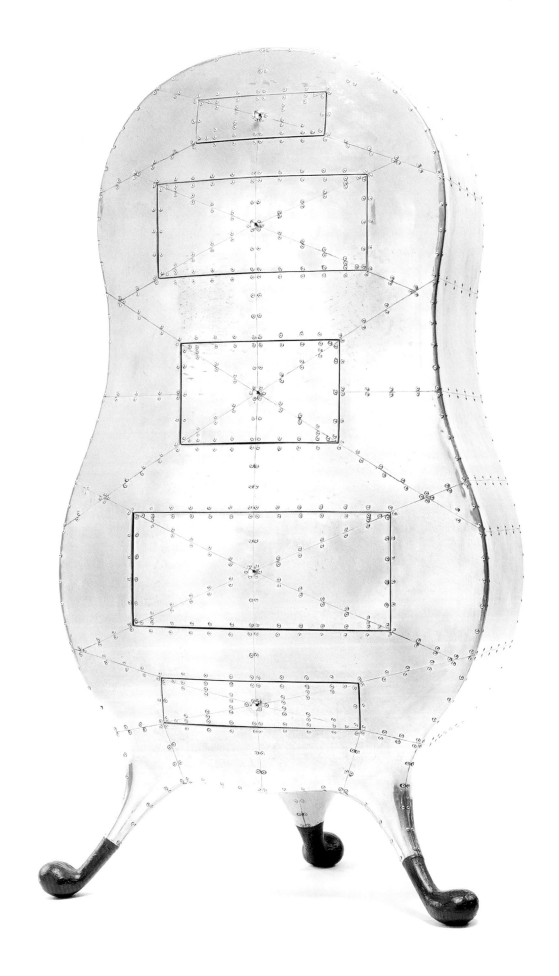

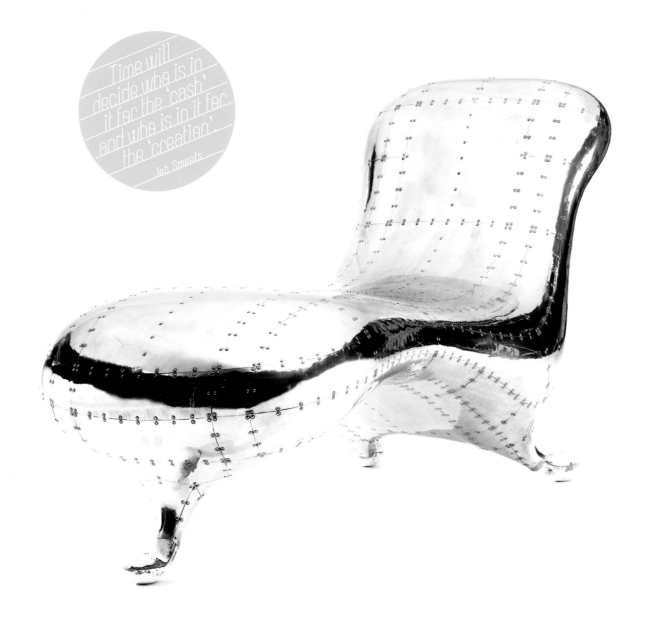

Marc Newson • Pod of Drawers
From an edition of 10 and 2 artist's proofs
Gallery: Sotheby's 20th Century Design
© Sotheby's 20th Century Design

Marc Newson • Lockheed Lounge Model No. MN-1LLW LC1
A prototype
Gallery: Sotheby's 20th Century Design
© Sotheby's 20th Century Design

Marc Newson • Event Horizon
Unique artist's proof
Gallery: Sotheby's 20th Century Design
© Sotheby's 20th Century Design

Albion

Previously known as Michel Hue-Williams Fine Art, the Albion gallery opened in London in 2004 with a programme of exhibitions and special projects. With a strong commitment to design, the gallery represents leading international artists including David Adjaye, Atelier Van Lieshout, Acconci Studio, and Humberto & Fernando Campana.

www.albion-gallery.com

Shay Alkalay / Raw Edges

(*1976) studied at the Politecnico di Milano, the Bezalel Art and Design Academy in Jerusalem and the Royal College of Art in London. He has a design company, Raw Edges, together with partner Yael Mer. Clients include: Arco, Established & Sons, Johnson Trading Gallery and Louise Blouin Media.

www.raw-edges.com

Raphaël von Allmen

(*1983) The Swiss designer graduated in industrial design from ECAL in 2007. He has worked with Nicolas Cortolezzi, Barber & Osgerby, Pierre Charpin, Florence Doléac, Jerzy Seymour and Martino d'Esposito. His work has been exhibited at the Centro Culturale Svizzero in Milan, L'Elac in Lausanne, the imm Cologne, Vienna Design Week, Basel World and the Vitra Store in New York, among others.

www.raphaelvonallmen.com

Tomás Alonso

(*1974) Spanish born Tomás Alonso studied Industrial Design at the Art Institute of Fort Lauderdale in Florida and the Royal College of Art in London. He is a member of the London based OKAY Studio group. He combines simple elements into more complex structures to furnish people with building blocks for creating their own environments.

www.tomas-alonso.com

gabrielle ammann // designer's gallery

Established in 2006 by the German interior architect and consultant Gabrielle Ammann and based in Cologne, Germany, the Designer's Gallery concentrates on the intersection between architecture, fine art and design. The gallery currently represents Ron Arad, Johanna Grawunder, Zaha Hadid, Shi Jianmin, Marc Newson, Satyendra Pakhalé, Lin Tianmiao and Zhang Wang.

www.designers-gallery.com

Aqua Creations

A design practice set up in 1994 by designer Ayala Serfaty (*1962) and photographer Albi Serfaty (*1960). Based in Tel Aviv with additional showrooms in New York and Shanghai, the design studio specialises in lighting and furniture lines as well as limited-edition custom designs. Clients include: Radisson SAS Hotel in Bucharest, MGM Mirage Casino, Planet Hollywood Casino and Hotel in Las Vegas, Palazzo di Brera in Milan, Cocoon Bar in London, Hotel Des Arts in Barcelona and the Mandarin Oriental Hotel in Tokyo.

www.aquagallery.com

Aram Gallery

An independently curated space that promotes the understanding of contemporary design by presenting experimental and new work of designers and artists, with a special interest in their early careers. Recent exhibitions have shown the works of Martino Gamper, Ron Arad, Pieke Bergmans, Sarah Wilson, Luis Eslava, Tom Dixon, El Ultimo Grito, Jessica Ogden, Stuart Haygarth, Jordi Canudas, Thomas Gardner, Stefano Giovannoni, Gitta Gschwendtner, Ronen Kadushin and Kazuhiro Yamanka, among others.

www.thearamgallery.org

Takashi Shinozaki / Asterisk Studio

(*1968) graduated in architecture from the Tokyo National University of Fine Arts and Music. In 1997 he established Asterisk Studio, and has exhibited his work at Tokyo Design Center, Salone del Mobile, Milan, the imm Cologne, the Good Design Award Winner's Show and the Tokyo Big Sight.

www.asterisk-studio.com

Maarten Baas

(*1978) Dutch designer Maarten Baas graduated from the Design Academy Eindhoven with a collection of furniture entitled Smoke, which immediately propelled him into the international limelight. His work continues to be acclaimed by museums, critics and collectors alike. In 2005, together with production manager Bas den Herder, he founded the design studio Baas & den Herder, which enables him to produce unique pieces on a large scale while still allowing them to be handcrafted in Holland.

www.maartenbaas.com

Emmanuel Babled

(*1967) graduated from the European Institute of Design in Milan. He started Studio Babled in 1995 in Milan, specialising in the development of industrial design products and objects in glass and crystal for companies such as Baccarat, Covo, Venini and Rosenthal. As a glass designer, Emmanuel Babled produces one-off and limited editions of design pieces, which have been shown in numerous exhibitions around the world.

www.babled.net

Markus Benesch

(1969*) has been an industrial and interior designer since 1989, working with companies such as Abet Laminati, Mövenpick Group, Paul Smith, Esselte Leitz and Rasch. His studio Markus Benesch Creates is based in Munich and Milan, and focuses on creating products, spaces, materials and surfaces. Benesch also holds seminars and workshops in interior design, product and communication design in Reims and Milan.

www.markusbenesch.com

Pieke Bergmans

(*1978) After studying graphics and 3D design, she turned to industrial design, graduating from the Design Academy Eindhoven and the Royal College of Art, London. She works in porcelain, plastic or glass, aiming to combine function, form and message in a single gesture. Based in Holland, Bergmans' client list includes Rosenthal, Fabrica Treviso, Charles Bergmans Shoe Design Studio, Studio Wanders Wonders and Design Studio Iglu Hong Kong.

www.piekebergmans.com

Jurgen Bey

(*1965) A graduate of the Design Academy Eindhoven, Jurgen Bey has helped to shape the image of Dutch design at an international level. He sees good art as scientific research that enables people to experience reality differently over and over again. Bey is a professor at the Hochschule für Bildende Künste in Karlsruhe, Germany, the Icelandic Academy in Reykjavik, and the Design Academy in Eindhoven, the Netherlands. He is also an advisor for SKOR (Amsterdam Committee for Art in Public Space) and art director of the design company Prooff.

www.jurgenbey.nl

Big-game

The three designers from Big-game, Elric Petit (B), Grégoire Jeanmonod (CH) and Augustin Scott de Martinville (F), met at ECAL University of Art & Design in Lausanne, where they studied industrial design together. In 2004 they founded the Big-game design studio, which is now based in Lausanne and Brussels. All three also teach design at ECAL and La Cambre in Brussels. While their approach is often experimental, an inherent industrial realism makes their products sustainable for the market, and some of their designs are produced by companies such as Ligne Roset, Mitralux, Vlaemsch and Domestic. Their motto: 'From confrontation comes progress'.

www.big-game.ch

Ronan and Erwan Bouroullec

(*1971) and (*1976) respectively. The Bouroullec brothers have worked together since 1999, collaborating with manufacturers such as Vitra, Cappellini, Issey Miyake, Magis, Ligne Roset, Habitat and the Kreo Gallery. Ronan graduated from the Ecole Nationale des Arts Décoratifs in Paris and initially began designing alone, but was later joined by Erwan, who studied at the Ecole des Beaux-Arts in Cergy-Pontoise. Known for creating designs that play with perceptions, their works have been exhibited at the London Design Museum, the Museum of Contemporary Art, Los Angeles, the Boijmans Museum of Art, Rotterdam and are included in the permanent collections of MoMA, New York, Centre Pompidou, Paris and the Lisbon Design Museum.

www.bouroullec.com

François Brument

(*1977) graduated from Ensci-Les Ateliers, France. He is a freelance designer and professor of digital creation at ESADSE Superior School of Art and Design in Saint-Etienne. He specialises in digital design, substituting drawing with data-processing programming, and develops design in perpetual change. His work is part of the French National Contemporary Art Fund collection.

www.in-flexions.com

Stephen Burks

(*1969) Burks's studio Readymade Projects, based in New York, designs projects ranging from retail interiors and events to packaging, consumer products, lighting, furniture and home accessories for international brands including Artecnica, B&B Italia, Boffi, Calvin Klein, Cappellini and Missoni. Burks has hosted design workshops at numerous international design schools and colleges, including ECAL in Lausanne, the Ecole Des Beaux Arts de Saint-Etienne, Konstfack in Stockholm, Parsons School of Design and the Pratt Institute in New York. In his commitment to sustainable design in the developing world he collaborates with the non-profit organisations Aid To Artisans and the Nature Conservancy.

www.readymadeprojects.com

Camp

After graduating in architecture and design, interior design and woodworking respectively, Atsushi Oohara, Miyuki Okada and Gen Kido worked together at Inoue Industries Co. in Tokyo before setting up their own company Camp in 2007. They describe Camp as 'an open-minded factory for users, designers and architects creating a little bit of future and fun'.

www.madeincamp.com

Fernando and Humberto Campana

(*1961) and (*1953) respectively. The Campana brothers are perhaps the most famous contemporary designers in South America. Humberto graduated in law from the University in São Paulo and Fernando in architecture from the São Paulo School of Fine Arts. They set up Estudio Campana in 1983, and make furniture and design objects based on everyday materials ranging from recycled remnants to soft toys and industrial plastics. Some of their works are manufactured by Edra and Cappellini and have been exhibited in galleries such as Albion, Vivid, Rove, The Apartment and Moss.

www.campanas.com.br

Nacho Carbonell

(*1980) graduated from the Spanish Cardenal Herrera-CEU University in 2003 and the Design Academy Eindhoven in 2007. As a designer/artist, he creates objects with his hands in order to give them his personality, and strives to add a fictional or fantasy element that allows them to escape everyday life. His work has been lauded by the media and professionals worldwide and exhibited at the Spazio Rossana Orlandi in Milan, the Salon del Mueble de Valencia, DesignHuis, Eindhoven and the Designersblock, Milan.

www.nachocarbonell.com

Wava Carpenter

is director of culture + content for Design Miami/Basel, orchestrating the show's programming, including the Design Talks, Design Performances, Satellite Exhibitions and Design Awards. Prior to joining Design Miami, Carpenter worked on exhibitions for Cooper-Hewitt, National Design Museum, including the exhibitions Second Skin and New Design from Israel. She has also taught critical theory classes at Parsons The New School for Design, where she studied for her Master's degree.

Carpenters Workshop Gallery

opened its first space in 2004 in an old gasworks in Chelsea and recently a second space in London's Mayfair. The gallery specialises in the converging fields of art and design, promoting contemporary designers through exhibiting unique and limited-edition works in solo and group exhibitions. Represented artists and designers include: Jurgen Bey, Ron Arad, Atelier van Lieshout, Ingrid Donat, Tejo Remy, Robert Stadler, Charles Trevelyan, Marcel Wanders, Pablo Reinoso, Demakersvan, Joris Laarman, Xavier Lust, Max Lamb, Sebastian Brajkovic, Vincent Dubourg and Ika Kuengel.

www.cwgdesign.com

Jeremy Cole

(*1973) A New Zealand-born, self-taught designer who was introduced to the world of design at the age of four in his mother's interior design show room. Cole's work draws on the forms of vegetables and flowers. His studio is based in London and work has been exhibited at the ICFF in New York, the Maison et Objet in Paris and 100% Design London.

www.jeremycole.net

Nick Compton

(*1968) is Features Director of Wallpaper magazine. He has written for a number of international magazines and newspapers including The Face, Arena, iD, Details, The Independent on Sunday, Observer and Sunday Telegraph. Compton has taken a special interest in the design art market and become a key commentator on its workings and development.

Contrasts Gallery

Founded in 1992 by Pearl Lam, Contrasts Gallery explores the relationship between art, architecture and design while celebrating and exaggerating differences. Lam aims to combine Western and Eastern influences on art and design and create a new aesthetic, showing antiques alongside the most cutting-edge designs of today. As well as hosting solo exhibitions by Chinese, American and European artists, the Shanghai-based gallery focuses on the cross-disciplinary aspects of art and design and a re-evaluation of Chinese contemporary art.

www.contrastsgallery.com

Charlie Davidson

(*1970) set up a design studio in east London after leaving college in 1993. He worked as a freelance concept designer for the Danish toy company LEGO and as an art director and set designer in television and fashion photography. In 1997 he began to focus on producing his own furniture and started exhibiting work under the label The Lander Project. Charlie Davidson Studio moved to Sweden in 2007, working on a number of commissions and producing furniture and lighting.

www.charlie-davidson.com

Design Drift

founded in 2006 by Ralph Nauta and Lonneke Gordijn, both graduates of the Design Academy Eindhoven, the Netherlands. The studio activities include product design as well as projects and concepts for interior and public space. Nauta and Gordijn work towards ecologically efficient and socially responsible business practice.

www.designdrift.nl

Design Miami/Basel

Founded in 2005 by design gallerist Ambra Medda and her partner, the Miami real estate magnate Craig Robins, in a few short years Design Miami/Basel has become one of the world's leading forums for international limited-edition design and design art. There are two shows annually: in Miami, Florida in December and Basel, Switzerland in June. They bring together the most influential designers, collectors, dealers, curators and critics from around the world and have had a considerable effect on the profile of limited-edition design.

www.designmiami.com/basel

Tom Dixon

(*1959) A self-taught product designer and interior decorator, Dixon has designed for companies including Asplund, Cappellini, Driade, Inflate, Moroso, Swarovski, Terence Conran and the fashion designers Jean Paul Gaultier, Ralph Lauren and Vivienne Westwood. In 1997 Dixon was appointed creative director of the UK furniture store Habitat, where he has reissued archive designs by Verner Panton, Ettore Sottsass and Robin Day, as well as commissioning new pieces from Ronan and Erwan Bouroullec, Ineke Hans and Marc Newson. He continues to work as an independent designer and as creative director of Artek, a Finnish furniture manufacturer. In 2002 Tom Dixon and David Begg set up the Tom Dixon design studio.

www.tomdixon.net

Evan Douglis

studied at Harvard Graduate School of Design and the Cooper Union, New York. He founded his architecture and interdisciplinary design firm Evan Douglis Studio in 1992, specialising in exhibitions, product design, installations, interiors and commercial building. He is currently the chief of the Undergraduate School of Architecture at the Pratt Institute. Prior to this he was the Director of Columbia University's Architecture Galleries and visiting professor at the Cooper Union.

www.evandouglis.com

Piet Hein Eek

(*1967) in Purmerend, the Netherlands. Piet Hein Eek creates unique products from 'worthless' material: waste material from industry and nature.

www.pietheineek.nl

Luis Eslava

(*1976) studied graphic and product design at the ESDI CEU in Valencia, web and multimedia design in the Istituto Europeo di Design in Madrid and product design at the Royal College of Art, London. He then returned to Valencia to set up his own studio, where he develops products and interiors for companies such as Okusa Ltd, Japan, ABR Produccion, Almerich Lighting, ICEX, Nani Marquina and others. His work has been exhibited worldwide.

www.luiseslava.com

Established & Sons

A British design and manufacturing company established in 2004 with a commitment to quality UK-based production, and to fostering and promoting the best of British design talent on an international platform. Established & Sons work with world-renowned designers as well as new talents, such as Barber Osgerby, Jasper Morrison, Maarten Baas, Amanda Levete, Raw Edges, and Zaha Hadid.

www.establishedandsons.com

Farmdesign

is a British design collective which produces a diverse range of 'engaging and witty' products. The four 'farmers' – Giles Miller, Alexena Cayless, Guy Brown and Sebastian Denver Hejna – draw inspiration from popular British culture. Hailed as rebel designers by Icon magazine, they are passionately committed to British manufacturing and quality craftsmanship.

www.farmdesign.co.uk

Rolf Fehlbaum

(*1941) chairman of the German furniture company Vitra, founded by his father Willi Fehlbaum in 1950. Fehlbaum studied social science at universities in Freiburg, Munich, Bern and Basel before setting up a publishing company for art books, producing documentaries in Munich and working as a consultant. In 1977 he took over as chairman from his father and began systematically expanding Vitra. His influence and active contribution to the development of design have been awarded with, amongst others, the IF Design Award and the Lucky Strike Designer Award of the Raymond Loewy Foundation.

Ryan Frank

A South African furniture designer living and working in East London. His collection of edgy free-range furniture makes frequent use of sustainable materials and draws inspiration from the urban landscape and his African roots. Ryan studied product design in Cape Town and Zwolle, The Netherlands. He worked for den Hartog Musch, a Dutch product design company and Alsop Architects before settling in London to concentrate on his own products.

www.ryanfrank.net

Freshwest Design

Marcus Beck (*1975) and Simon Macro (*1975), both studied fine art at the Manchester Metropolitan University and University of Brighton respectively. After graduating Beck concentrated on the production of limited-edition furniture whilst Macro worked with designer Thomas Heatherwick. In 2005 they established Freshwest Design which embraces both experimental and functional design.

www.freshwest.co.uk

Friedman Benda

was founded in New York City in 2007 by Barry Friedman and Marc Benda as a venue for cutting-edge art and design. The gallery features a programme of rotating exhibitions of contemporary work by some of the world's leading artists, architects and designers, including Ron Arad, Ettore Sottsass, Gaetano Pesce, Joris Laarman, Atelier van Lieshout, Zhang Huan, Nendo, and Front Design.

www.friedmanbenda.com

Front Design

are Sofia Lagerkvist, Charlotte von der Lancken, Anna Lindren, and Katja Sävström. Established in 2003, this quartet of Swedish industrial designers has a particular approach to design, often giving credit for its products to animals, physics, surroundings and materials. Front Design's works have been exhibited at the Salone del Mobile, Milan, Design Miami/Basel, Swarovski Crystal Palace and Tokyo's Chocolate exhibition. Front has worked with Droog Design as well as manufacturers such as Moooi and Coin.

www.frontdesign.se

Gagosian Gallery

is a big contemporary art gallery with seven locations: three in New York, one in Beverly Hills, two in London, and one in Rome. Its owner, the influential Larry Gagosian, is one of the most enigmatic personalities in the art dealer scene, and made his name dealing works by Jeff Koons, Ed Ruscha and Richard Serra. Exhibitions at the Gagosian galleries have included works by artists such as Andy Warhol, Damien Hirst, Tracey Emin, Jasper Johns, Nan Goldin, Richard Wright, Martin Kippenberger, Julian Schnabel, Cy Twombly, and Alberto Giacometti. His Marc Newson show in 2007 marked his entry into the design field.

www.gagosian.com

Galerie Italienne

Based in Paris, the Galerie Italienne was first opened in 2003 by owner Alessandro Pron and is dedicated to the promotion of Italian design through the production of new collections and the exhibition of contemporary furniture, highlighting synergies between art and design. Artists represented include: Mattia Bonetti, Johanna Grawunder, Nando Vigo and Marco Zanuso Jr.

www.galerieitalienne.com

Galerie Kreo

Founded in 1999, this Paris-based gallery is dedicated to artistic exploration in design. Husband and wife owners Didier and Clémence Krzentowski call Kreo a 'research laboratory' and the gallery is very much at the forefront of contemporary limited-edition design. They work closely with their stable of artists and designers, who regularly create exclusive editions both for and with the gallery. Designers who work with Kreo include: Ronan & Erwan Bouroullec, Pierre Charpin, Hella Jongerius, Jasper Morrison, Big-game, Front Design, Konstantin Grcic and Martin Szekely.

www.galeriekreo.com

Gallery Libby Sellers

Established in 2007 by the former London Design Museum curator, Libby Sellers, the gallery operates as a guerrilla gallery, promoting and supporting emerging design in temporary locations internationally. Represented designers include Stuart Haygarth, Simon Heijdens, Max Lamb, Julia Lohmann, Peter Marigold and Adrien Rovero.

www.libbysellers.com

Sarah van Gameren

graduated from the Design Academy Eindhoven, the Netherlands in 2004 and the Royal College of Art, London in 2006. She explores issues of mass production, consumption and accidental aesthetics within design, and investigates the value of design in search of a new definition. Her works have been presented at the Milan furniture fair and various exhibitions in Tokyo, London and across the Netherlands. She was also Designer in Residence at the Design Museum, London. In 2008 she set up Studio Glithero together with Tim Simpson.

www.sarahvangameren.com

Martino Gamper

(*1971) The Italian designer studied sculpture and product design at the University of Applied Arts and the Academy of Fine Arts in Vienna, and graduated from the Royal College of Art, London in 2000. That same year he set up his own practice. Gamper designs and produces a wide range of objects from limited-edition to semi-industrial products and site-specific installations. His work has been exhibited at the Victoria & Albert Museum, London, the London Design Museum, Sotheby's, Nilufar, Aram gallery and the MAK in Vienna.

www.gampermartino.com

David Gill

The David Gill Galleries 'blur the boundaries between applied and fine arts'. The current stable of designers includes Zaha Hadid, Fredrikson Stallard, Mattia Bonetti, Nigel Coates and Barnaby Barford. Known as a leading producer and dealer of contemporary design, David Gill opened his first gallery on Fulham Road, London, in 1987. He started off showing pieces by names such as Charlotte Perriand, Jean Prouvé, J. E. Ruhlmann and Eileen Gray, later adding Donald Judd, Yves Klein, Tom Dixon and Ron Arad. In 1989, Gill produced his first collection with Elisabeth Garouste and Mattia Bonetti, and since then has done collections with other designers including Jasper Morrison and Marc Newson.

www.davidgillgalleries.com

Johanna Grawunder

(*1961) is a designer and architect based in Milan and San Francisco. Graduating in architecture from California Polytechnic State University in San Luis Obispo, she completed her final year of studies in Florence and then moved to Milan. From 1985 to 2001 Grawunder worked in partnership with Ettore Sottsass, where she co-designed many of the firm's most prestigious projects. She set up her own studio in 2001. Her works span a broad range of projects and scales, from architecture and interiors to limited-edition furniture and lights for various galleries in Europe and the USA. She also collaborates on products with a few selected companies, including Flos, Boffi, B&B Italia, and Salviati.

www.grawunder.com

Konstantin Grcic

(*1965) founded Konstantin Grcic Industrial Design (KGID) in 1991. The Munich-based company specialises in various fields of design, ranging from furniture and industrial products to exhibition design and architecture-related work. KGID works with some of the leading names of the international design industry. Grcic's products have received a number of international design awards, and form part of the permanent collections of MoMA, New York, Centre Georges Pompidou, Paris and Die Neue Sammlung, Munich, among others.

www.konstantin-grcic.com

Ineke Hans

(*1966) graduated in 3D design from the Hogeschool voor de Kunsten in Arnhem and in furniture design from the Royal College of Art, London. She worked freelance for Habitat before setting up her own studio in 1998. Ineke Hans's work has evolved in many ways, combining the identity of a designer with the impulses of a sculptor and the industrial experience needed to define products with a commercial life.

www.inekehans.com

Stuart Haygarth

(*1966) studied graphic design and photography at Exeter College of Art & Design in Devon, England. After a few years spent as a photographic assistant and illustrator, he started working on design projects revolving around collections of objects and the transformation of their meaning. His works include chandeliers made of old spectacles or party poppers, installations, functional and sculptural objects.

www.stuarthaygarth.com

Matthew Hilton

(*1957) graduated in furniture design from Kingston Polytechnic and worked as an industrial designer for the London-based product design company Capa. He set up the Matthew Hilton Design Studio in 1985 and started working for the British retailer and manufacturer SCP, followed by commissions for manufacturers such as Driade, Disform, the Bradley Collection and Authentics.

www.matthewhilton.com

Graham Hudson

A sculpture graduate of Chelsea College of Art & Design and the Royal College of Art in London, Hudson uses a variety of media and materials including discarded furniture, pound store plastics, home and garden decor, turntables, fans, bin bags, lighting, a lot of screws, cable ties and tape. He has exhibited at the Locust Projects, Miami, Wall Space, New York, the Rokeby Gallery, the Saatchi Gallery and Gagosian in London.

www.rokebygallery.com

Richard Hutten

(*1967) graduated from the Design Academy Eindhoven, the Netherlands in 1991. That same year he started his own design studio, working on furniture, product, interior and exhibition design. He is one of the most internationally successful contemporary Dutch designers and a founding member of Droog Design. His work is in the permanent collections of the Centraal Museum, Utrecht, the Stedelijk Museum of Modern Art, Amsterdam, the Vitra Museum, Weil am Rhein and the San Francisco Museum of Modern Art. Hutten's clients include Hidden, E&Y Tokyo, Pure Design Toronto, Moss, Donna Karan and Karl Lagerfeld.

www.richardhutten.com

Johnson Trading Gallery

Paul Johnson made his name as owner and operator of Phurniture Inc., New York, a showroom founded in 2001 and dedicated solely to 20th-century modern furniture. An interest in contemporary artists and designers who push the boundaries when it comes to traditional furniture design, construction and production led Johnson to open the Johnson Trading Gallery in New York in 2007. The gallery is committed to commissioning and funding unique contemporary works from emerging artists, designers and architects, as well as curating exhibitions of 20th-century design. Represented designers include Max Lamb, Aranda/Lasch and Steven Holl Architects.

www.johnsontradinggallery.com

Hella Jongerius

(*1963) is known for the special way she fuses industry and craft, high and low tech, tradition and the contemporary. After graduating from the Design Academy Eindhoven in 1993, she started her design company, Jongeriuslab, through which she produces her own projects and pieces for clients such as Maharam, Royal Tichelaar Makkum, Vitra and IKEA. Her work has been shown at various museums and galleries, including the Cooper Hewitt National Design Museum, Moss Gallery and MoMA in New York, the Design Museum, London and Galerie Kreo in Paris.

www.jongeriuslab.com

Joost & Kiki

The Dutch duo Joost van Bleiswijk (*1976) and Kiki van Eijk (*1978) are partners who design autonomously, but also collaborate on projects intrinsically linked through craftsmanship and traditional techniques. Both are graduates of the Design Academy Eindhoven and have generated their own collections as well as working to commission for leading companies. Kiki van Eijk's client list includes: Moooi, Swarovski, Studio Edelkoort Paris, and Joost van Bleiswijk's: Ahrend, Bruut furniture, the city of Eindhoven and Lebesque.

www.kikiworld.nl

www.joostvanbleiswijk.com

Jousse Entreprise

Based in Paris, this art gallery is owned by Philippe Jousse, who for more than 25 years has contributed to the growing recognition of designers such as Jean Prouvé, Charlotte Perriand, Le Corbusier, Pierre Jeanneret, Georges Jouve and Jean Royère. Jousse Entreprise comprises three galleries in Paris: one focusing on architects' furniture from the 1950s, the second on fur-niture from the 1970s, and the third on contemporary art.

www.jousse-entreprise.com

Kayser+Metzner

Aylin Kayser (*1982) and Christian Metzner (*1983) are students of product design at the Fachhochschule Potsdam, Germany. They have already worked together on a number of projects, which have been exhibited at the imm Cologne, Light & Building Messe in Frankfurt and the DMY Berlin. They were awarded a Special Mention at the Light & Building Messe Frankfurt and a Top 10 nomination at the DMY Berlin.

aylinkayser@yahoo.de
info@christian-metzner.com

Pierre Keller

(*1945) trained in graphic design and has worked as a photographer, exhibition maker, publisher and art consultant for the last 20 years. Since 1995 he has been director of the l'Ecole cantonale d'art de Lausanne (ECAL) and is founder of L'Elac, a gallery for contemporary art in Lausanne. From 2000 to 2002 he was head of the Directors' Conference of Swiss Schools and Colleges for Design and since 2002 has been a member of the directors' committee of the HES-SO. In 2000 he was appointed an Officier des Arts et des Lettres of the French Republic.

www.ecal.ch

Kram/Weisshaar

Founded in 2002 by Reed Kram and Clemens Weisshaar with offices based in Munich and Stockholm. The studio designs spaces, products and media. Their products stand for a new form of integrated product and process development, and thus for a new way of thinking in design. Clients include: Prada, Rem Koolhaas, Authentics, Classicon, Moroso and Nymphenburg. Their work is included in the collections of the Centre Pompidou, Paris, the Vitra Design Museum, Weil am Rhein, and the Pinakothek der Moderne, Munich.

www.kramweisshaar.com

Joris Laarman

(*1979) graduated from the Design Academy Eindhoven in 2003 and went straight on to set up his studio. A conceptual and poetic approach to product design and architecture has secured him numerous awards, including Wallpaper's young designer of the year, the Red Dot Design Award, Woon Award and the international Elle Decoration talent of the year 2008. He has worked with industrial design companies such as Flos, Vitra, Swarovski and Droog, as well as galleries such as Friedman Benda and Haunch of Venison.

www.jorislaarman.com

Max Lamb

(*1980) A native Cornwall, Lamb graduated in 3D design from Northumbria University in 2003. The same year he began working for Ou Baholyodhin Studio in London, where he designed furniture, graphics and interior products and spaces for restaurants, shops and exhibitions. He completed his Master's degree in design products at the Royal College of Arts, London in 2006. After a year designing for Tom Dixon Studio, Lamb established his own company and currently teaches in the Industrial Design Department at ECAL.

www.maxlamb.org

Mathieu Lehanneur

(*1974) graduated from Ensci-Les Ateliers in 2001 before establishing his own studio for product and exhibition design projects. His focus lies on the exploration of possibilities and their functional potential in nature and technology. Lehanneur is also the postgraduate research manager at Cité du Design / École des Beaux-Arts de Saint-Etienne, France.

www.mathieulehanneur.com

Arik Levy

(*1963) is an industrial designer and co-founder of the firm L Design, together with Pippo Lionni. Levy graduated from the Art Center College of Design, La Tour-de-Peilz, Switzerland. He has taught at the Ensci-Les Ateliers in Paris and led design workshops at various design schools in Europe. His work has been exhibited at the Centre Georges Pompidou in Paris, the Victoria & Albert Museum in London and the Pascale Cottard-Ollsson Gallery in Stockholm.

www.ariklevy.fr

Khai Liew

(*1952) Before designing his own furniture pieces, Khai Liew was a specialist valuer, conservator and consultant in early Australian furniture for over 20 years. This experience was the principal factor in the formation and development of his own design vocabulary. His aesthetic does not represent a desire for perfection, but rather a quest for a certain rhythm, a poetry of form that captures the balance of air and substance, light and shade.

www.khailiewdesign.com

Gudrun Lilja

studied furniture making at the Reykjavik School of Industry, Iceland and 'man and living' at the Design Academy Eindhoven. After a brief internship at Studio Jurgen Bey, Gudrun Lilja Gunnlaugsdóttir desiged the Husavik Whale Museum in Iceland. In 2005 she set up Studio Bility together with Olafur Omarsson and Jon Asgeir Hreinsson. Her work has been widely exhibited, both individually and as part of the team.

www.bility.is

Winnie Lui

(*1981) graduated from Central Saint Martins College, London in fashion communication and promotion. Based in Hong Kong, the jewellery designer Winnie Lui creates tailor-made necklaces, brooches and chapeaux, and also works in the fields of interior design, graphics, photography and installation. Her latest project is a limited-edition chandelier designed for the UK-based company Innermost.

www.winnielui.com

Lund University students

31 industrial design students from the Lund University in Sweden worked together on a project entitled 'What can you bring to the table?' inspired by the game where you sketch part of a character on a piece of paper, fold it over and pass on to another person to draw the next part without seeing what was drawn before. The aim was to design chairs, each representing a different characteristic. The resulting five chairs — entitled vain, awkward, voluptuous, androgynous and vicious — were shown at the Zona Tortona in Milan in 2008.

www.whatcanyoubringtothetable.com

Magen H Gallery

Since 1997, Magen H Gallery XX Century Design has shown innovative designers in the decorative arts, sculpture, architecture and ceramics, with particular emphasis on French post-war designers. The collection reflects an artistic dialogue between historically significant works and contemporaries who visually articulate a personal philosophy. In addition to the permanent space in New York, Magen H Gallery exhibits annually at Design Miami/Basel, Design London, and Art Basel.

www.magenxxcentury.com

Geoffrey Mann

This Scottish product artist creates unique pieces of art that often incorporate light sources. Mann's works are made using rapid prototyping, a plaster composite and glass. He graduated in ceramics and glass from the Royal College of Art in 2005 and founded Studio*Mrmann that same year. His critically acclaimed Long Exposure and Natural Occurrence series have been exhibited internationally.

www.mrmann.co.uk

Eva Marguerre

(*1983) studies product design at the Hochschule für Gestaltung in Karlsruhe, Germany. She has worked as an intern at the Luigi Colani studio and for Stefan Diez, and as creative director for interior magazines such as Brigitte, Schöner Wohnen and Living at Home. Her work has been exhibited at Luminale and the Tendence fairs in Frankfurt, the imm Cologne, Interieur in Belgium and the International Festival of Design in Lodz.

www.eva-marguerre.de

Peter Marigold

(*1974) lives and works in London and is part of the OKAY Studio team. He studied at Central Saint Martins College of Art and Design and the Royal College of Art in London. His work has been exhibited at the FAT galerie, Paris, the Libby Sellers gallery, the Design Museum, London and MoMA, New York. With his Make/Shift shelving project Peter Marigold was shortlisted for Designer of the Year 2008 at the Design Museum in London.

www.petermarigold.com

Laurent Massaloux

(*1968) graduated from the Ensci-Les Ateliers in 1991 and co-founded Radi Designers in 1992. Massaloux concentrates on research projects including prototypes and limited editions in various fields. He has exhibited at: ToolsGalerie, Galerie Via and Salon du Meuble de Paris, among others.

www.massaloux.net

Julian Mayor

is an artist and designer based in East London. After graduating from the Royal College of Art in 2000 he worked for IDEO design, Pentagram and other studios whilst exhibiting his own work at the FAT Galerie in Paris, Spazio Rossana Orlandi in Milan, Tokyo Design Festival, London Design Festival and MoMA in New York. He is currently teaching 3D computer modelling at the London College of Communication and continuing his exploration of computers and sculptural form.

www.julianmayor.com

Meta

Established by its parent company Mallet, an antique house specialising in 18th-century furniture and objects, Meta creates timeless contemporary objects and furniture of exceptional quality. A group of leading designers, including Asymptote, Edward Barber & Jay Osgerby, Tord Boontje, Matali Crasset and Wales & Wales, were commissioned in association with over 50 master ateliers and artisans to create Meta's inaugural collection, launched during the Salone del Mobile in Milan in April 2008. Giles Hutchinson-Smith is the managing director of both Meta and Mallet.

www.madebymeta.com

Minale-Maeda

Japanese-born Kuniko Maeda and Italian-born, German-reared Mario Minale met at the Design Academy Eindhoven, the Netherlands, after studying at Musashino Art University, Tokyo and the University of Wuppertal, Germany, respectively. In 2005 they formed their Minale-Maeda design studio based in Rotterdam. They design from a conceptual angle on topics of contemporary culture, both self-initiated and on commission. Their works have been exhibited at the ToolsGalerie in Paris, the Salone Satellite in Milan, 100% East in London and the travelling exhibition of Droog Design.

www.minale-maeda.com

mitterrand + cramer

Established by Edward Mitterrand and Stéphanie Cramer in 2007, the gallery essentially focuses on art dealing and consulting activities. However, the response to their first design exhibition, held at the end of 2007 and featuring Atelier Oï, Ron Arad, Maarten Baas, Studio Job and Marcel Wanders amongst others, encouraged the gallery to hold a year dedicated to design the following year.

www.mitterrand-cramer.com

Moss

Former fashion entrepreneur Murray Moss opened his shop Moss in a small gallery space in Soho in 1994, determined to transform the public perception of industrial product design. The furniture and objects offered at the shop deliberately blur the distinctions between production and craft, between industry and art, and more recently, between industrial and decorative arts. Moss has been instrumental in shaping the direction of design retail, and the shop functions as arbiter, advocate and presenter, as well as gallery, showroom and salon.
www.mossonline.com

Helen Amy Murray

(*1980) studied textiles at Chelsea College of Art and Design. She creates leather-upholstered furniture decorated with her own patented form of cut surface reliefs. She set up her own label in 2003, working primarily to commission. Murray has exhibited at the Arums Gallery, Paris, the Victoria & Albert Museum, 100% Design London and the Royal College of Art.
www.helenamymurray.com

Oscar Narud

Studied art and design at Central Saint Martins College of Art and Design and the Royal College of Art, from which he graduated with a Master's in product design in 2006. Narud has worked freelance for El Ultimo Grito and Nigel Coates Studio and is a founding member of the design collective OKAY Studio based in London. His work has been exhibited in solo and group exhibitions at the Aram Gallery in London, the Zeus gallery in Milan and the Istituto Europeo di Design in Madrid.
www.oscarnarud.com

Gareth Neal

(*1974) graduated in furniture design and craftsmanship from Buckinghamshire College, UK. From his studio in east London he designs and produces contemporary furniture, specialising in one-off and limited-edition pieces for individual clients and companies. Gareth Neal's furniture has been exhibited around the world, from Sotheby's in New York to the Victoria & Albert Museum in London.
www.garethneal.co.uk

Nendo

Founded in Tokyo in 2002 by architect Oki Sato, the company's goal is to bring small surprises to people through a multidisciplinary practice including architecture, interiors, furniture, industrial products and graphic design. In 2005 the company opened its second office in Milan. Nendo's client list includes Cappellini, DePadova, Issey Miyake, Kenzo Parfums, Toyota, Puma and Nec.
www.nendo.jp

Marc Newson

(*1963) works across a wide range of disciplines, creating everything from chairs, household objects, bicycles and concept cars to restaurants, recording studios and interiors of private and commercial jets. His long client list includes: Flos, Cappellini, Moroso, Magis, B&B Italia and Quantas Airways. After studying jewellery and sculpture at the Sydney College of the Arts he spent four years in Tokyo, before setting up his own studio in Paris in 1991, followed by Marc Newson Ltd in London in 1997. His works are present in most major permanent museum collections including the MoMA in New York, London's Design Museum, Centre Georges Pompidou and the Vitra Design Museum.
www.marc-newson.com

Wouter Nieuwendijk

(*1978) graduated in industrial design from the Gerrit Rietveld Academie, Amsterdam, the Netherlands. He founded the HUH design studio in 2006 together with Suzanne van Oirschot, Karel, David Graas, Laura de Monchy and Nienke Sybrandy.
www.checkhuh.nl

Nilufar

Founded in 1979 by Nina Yashar Nilufar, this is one of Italy's most active and original galleries in the fields of historical design, antique oriental carpets and furniture. The gallery exhibitions mix historical design objects with Nilufar editions by designers such as Alessandro Mendini, Philippe Bestenheider, Arik Levy, Caturegil & Formica, Barnaba Fornasetti, Andrea Salvetti, Sarah Van Gameren, Martino Gamper, Tim Simpson and Julia Lohman.
www.nilufar.com

Suzanne van Oirschot

(*1976) After training to be a jewellery designer, van Oirschot studied at the Art Academy of Maastricht and the Sandberg Institute in Amsterdam. She founded the HUH design studio in 2006 together with Wouter Nieuwendijk, Karel, David Graas, Laura de Monchy and Nienke Sybrandy.
www.checkhuh.nl

Rick Owens

is an American fashion and furniture designer based in Paris. He started his fashion label in the early 1990s after dropping out of art school, and held his first show in New York in 2001. He won a CFDA New Talent award a year later. Owens introduced his first furniture collection in 2005, inspired by his favourite shapes, from Eileen Grey to Brancusi and California skate parks. He is represented by Jousse Entreprise.
www.rickowens.eu

Satyendra Pakhalé

(*1967) studied engineering and design in India and advanced product design in Switzerland. Pakhalé created products and scenarios for new business creations at Philips Design before setting up his own design practice based in Amsterdam in 1998. Since then he has worked for companies such as Alessi, Bosa, Cappellini, C-Sam, Cor Unum, Curvet, Väveriet and Moroso. His prime interest is the design of mass-producible, technically challenging personal products, from objects to transport systems and limited-edition pieces.
www.satyendra-pakhale.com

Alexander Payne

set up the design department of Phillips de Pury & Company in 1999 and is now a partner in the firm, holding sales in both London and New York. His career started at the Hampton Fine Art in Godalming, followed by five years at Bonham's, London, where he was head of the 20th-century design department. Payne has contributed to and written various books on design, including The Coffee Table Coffee Table Book (with James Zemaitis), 1000 Lights Volumes 1&2, Collecting Modern Design and Series Books Design.

Perimeter Editions

Since 2004 Perimeter has been developing, producing and promoting furniture and objects with international designers of different generations. The company actively supports international designers such as Adrien Gardère and Guillaume Bardet (France), James Lethbridge (UK), Studio Libertiny (Netherlands), as well as new talents from Africa.
www.perimeter-editions.com

Gaetano Pesce

(*1939) is an architect-artist-designer based in New York City. He has worked in a range of fields including architecture, urban planning, interior, exhibition and industrial design. He studied architecture at the University of Venice and is now a visiting lecturer and professor at many institutions in America and abroad, including the Cooper Union in New York and the Institut d'Architecture et d'Etudes Urbaines in Strasbourg, France. He received the Chrysler Award for Innovation and Design in 1993.
www.gaetanopesce.com

Gord Peteran

(*1956) is a Toronto-based artist who creates site-specific works of art and furniture for public and private spaces. Influenced by a variety of sources, including historical furniture makers and the work of historical and contemporary painters, Peteran has created a wide range of work, including functional and one-of-a-kind pieces that he makes in both metal and wood, describing it as his 'paints and brushes'.

Olivier Peyricot

(*1969) a graduate of ESDI (Ecole Supérieure de Design Industriel) in Paris, Olivier Peyricot is a designer, writer and teacher at the Ecole Nationale des Arts Décoratifs in Paris. His work has been shown in numerous exhibitions, including MoMA New York, Centre Pompidou, ToolsGalerie and the Fond National d'Art Moderne. He has designed interiors and objects for Edra, Range Camp Hotel, ATR and others.
www.olivierpeyricot.com

Phillips de Pury & Company

Founded in London in 1796 and known then as Phillips', this traditional auction house has held sales for many distinguished collectors. It remained a family company until 1999, when Phillips, Son & Neale was bought by Bernard Arnault, the chairman of Louis Vuitton Moët Hennessy (LVMH) who shortly after merged with the private art dealers Simon de Pury and Daniela Luxembourg. In 2002 de Pury & Luxembourg took majority control of the company, and in 2003 Simon de Pury moved the headquarters under the name Phillips de Pury & Company to the Meatpacking district in Chelsea, New York, where it now focuses exclusively on the sale of contemporary art, design, jewellery and photography.
www.phillipsdepury.com

Russell Pinch

(*1973) After graduating from Ravensbourne College of Design, UK he worked as Sir Terence Conran's design assistant and became a senior product designer for the Conran Group. Five years later he co-founded The Nest, a multidisciplinary brand design agency with clients including British Airways, MFI, WHSmith, Rip Curl and Selfridges. In 2004, with his wife Oona Bannon, he founded Pinch, a furniture, product and interior design company. That year they launched their first collection at 100% Design and received the Blueprint Best Newcomer 2004 Award.
www.pinchdesign.com

POSTFOSSIL

The group POSTFOSSIL was founded in 2007 by a collective of ten young Swiss designers: Anna Blattert, Annina Gähwiler, Christine Birkhoven, Claudia Heiniger, Corina Zuberbühler, Daniel Gafner, Florian Hauswirth, Isabelle Hauser, Michael Niederberger and Thomas Walde. This is a platform for designers to discuss current issues surrounding design and the ways in which they can respond to it. For their first collection, presented at the Salone Satellite in Milan in 2008, the design collective received the Design Report award.
www.postfossil.ch

Tom Price

(*1973) studied product design at the Royal College of Art, London after studying sculpture at the Bath College of Higher Education and furniture design & realisation at the London Metropolitan University. For his works, which he designs with a distinctly sculptural aesthetic in mind, he has received the Boss Design Mentoring Award and the Peter Walker Award for Innovation in Furniture Design.
www.tom-price.com

Diego Ramos

(*1978) graduated in industrial design from Eina School of Arts and Design, Barcelona and the Royal College of Art in London. In 2006 he established the Diego Ramos Studio, based in Barcelona, Madrid and London. His work has been shown in exhibitions at the Museum of Contemporary Art of Barcelona, the Decorative Arts Museum, Barcelona, the 300% Spanish Design at Centro Dragão do Mar de Arte e Cultura in Brazil and Tyvek World.
www.diegoramos.es

Pablo Reinoso

(*1955) is a French-Argentine artist and designer living and working in Paris since 1979. A self-taught sculptor, he took courses in architecture at Buenos Aires University. For a long time he worked mainly with wood, slate, marble, brass and steel before deciding to extend his practice to other materials. He combines his work as sculptor and designer, reinterpreting furniture and placing it in new paradigms.

www.pabloreinoso.com

Tejo Remy

(*1969) works as an independent product and interior designer in Utrecht, often in collaboration with Rene Veenhuizen. A lot of their work has been exhibited at the Galeries nationales du Grand Palais in Paris, the ACME in Los Angeles, the Carpenters Workshop Gallery, the Centre d'Art Passerelle in Brest and the MoMA in San Francisco. Remy is a central figure at Droog Design and teaches at the Hogeschool voor de Kunsten Utrecht, the Netherlands.

www.remyveenhuizen.nl

Dylan Kehde Roelofs

originally trained as a scientific glassblower and attended the Pilchuck glass school in Washington, USA as well as a half dozen other universities. He designs and fabricates the plasma neon tubes for the Man at the annual Burning Man Festival, and is a 'practising alchemist and daguerreotypist'.

www.incandescentsculpture.com

Frédéric Ruyant

(*1961) is an architect and designer who focuses on the creation of furniture and objects as well as product and space design for brands such as Issey Miyake, Ligne Roset, Ministère de la culture, Galerie Lafayette, ToolsGalerie, Hôtel Costes, Moët et Chandon, LVMH, Jean Paul Gaultier and Baccarat. Ruyant founded his own agency in 1996.

www.fredericruyant.com

Karen Ryan

studied 3D design at the Design and Fine Art University of Portsmouth and product design at the Royal College of Art. Since 2001 Ryan has exhibited her work at the Designersblock and 100% East in London, the Spazio Rossana Orlandi in Milan and other international galleries. She is a recipient of the Aspex Gallery Designer Maker Award.

www.bykarenryan.co.uk

Tomek Rygalik

(*1976) studied architecture at the Technical University of Lodz, Poland and industrial design at the Pratt Institute in New York. After several collaborations with companies including Kodak, Polaroid, MTV and DuPont he went to the Royal College of Art in London before establishing his own design practice in London in 2005. He is now a research associate at the RCA and teaches at the Academy of Fine Arts in Warsaw. Recent clients include: Moroso, Artek, IKER, Noti, ABR, Heal's and Ideal Standard.

www.tomekrygalik.com

Rolf Sachs

(*1955) studied business administration in London and San Francisco before focusing on furniture design 20 years ago. As a well-known designer/artist recognised for his distinctive approach, he has had a number of solo and group exhibitions in the USA, Germany, Italy, Belgium, Austria and the UK. His works are inspired by the world of fine rather than decorative arts, focusing on the conceptual rather than the decorative aspects, with an added touch of humour.

www.rolfsachs.com

Kenny Schachter / ROVE

In 2001 Kenny Schachter conTEMPorary opened on New York's Charles Lane, hosting shows by names like Mary Heilmann, Dennis Oppenheim and Vito Acconci. In October 2004 Kenny Schachter relocated to London and opened ROVE on Hoxton Square in the East End, occupying a site that will be redeveloped shortly by Zaha Hadid Architects to provide a permanent home for the gallery. Since opening in London, ROVE has presented shows drawing on an international selection of designers and artists including Zaha Hadid, Keith Coventry, Arik Levy, Vito Acconci and William Pope.L.

www.rovetv.net

Sotheby's

Founded in 1744, Sotheby's is now the world's largest auction house, covering all areas of the fine and decorative arts. The company has headquarters in London and New York, as well as offices in all major cities across Europe, the United States, Canada and Asia. In 2000 Sotheby's also became the first international art auction house to hold auctions on the Internet via the eBay live auctions service. A recent expansion of the New York headquarters has resulted in a 10th-floor gallery that is now an exhibition space for art and design.

www.sothebys.com

Studio Hausen

Jörg Höltje (*1981) and Joscha Brose (*1981) are currently studying industrial design at the University of Applied Arts in Berlin and working freelance for the Dan Pearlman design agency. Höltje spent four months as an intern at the Design Studio Patricia Urquiola, while Brose did an internship with the sports brand Orca in Hong Kong. They founded Studio Hausen in 2006. Although they are still students, they have already exhibited their work at the imm Cologne and the Salone del Mobile in Milan twice. Their Serpentine lamp is in production with Ligne Roset.

www.studiohausen.com

Studio Job

Founded in 1997 by Job Smeets (*1970) and Nynke Tynagel (*1977), both graduates of the Design Academy Eindhoven. Right from the start their collaboration resulted in highly expressive, usually one-off or limited-edition artisan works. Studio Job has worked with various manufacturers, including Swarovski, Royal Tichelaar Makkum, Moooi, and has exhibited at the MoMA, New York, the Victoria & Albert Museum, London, and the Centraal Museum, Utrecht and the Groninger Museum, the Netherlands.

www.studiojob.be

Swarovski

Established in 1895 by Daniel Swarovski, the company is the world's leading producer of precision-cut crystal for fashion, jewellery, lighting, interiors and architecture. Based in Wattens, Austria and run by fourth- and fifth-generation family members, the company comprises two major divisions: one producing and selling loose crystals to the industry, and the other creating design-driven finished products. In 2002 Nadja Swarovski introduced the Swarovski Crystal Palace event, which invited leading designers to reinvent the chandelier using Swarovski crystals. It has now expanded into an annual collaboration where designers are commissioned to create contemporary interpretations of lighting, furniture and design. The results are shown during the Salone del Mobile in Milan, Paris Fashion Week and Design Miami/Basel.

www.swarovskisparkles.com

ToolsGalerie

was created in 2003 as a venue for research and convergence with the aim of promoting the work of contemporary designers. Producing limited editions of objects and furniture for its exhibitions, ToolsGalerie works with established designers and new talents including Maarten Baas, Jurgen Bey, Fredrikson Stallard, Joris Laarman, Hella Jongerius, Richard Hutten, Ineke Hans, Laurent Massaloux and Marcel Wanders.

www.toolsgalerie.com

Marcus Tremonto

The American designer/artist set up his New York-based Treluce Studios with wife and partner Monica Tremonto in 2002. He initially studied maths and physics and worked as an engineer before switching to art and design. Tremonto works with electroluminescent materials to create forms and pieces that take light out of the realm of the functional. International recognition for his limited-edition Lightworks pieces led to a one-man show at Phillips de Pury & Company in 2007 and was followed by a project for the Swarovski Crystal Palace in Milan in 2008. As a consultant Tremonto has also been an influential figure in the design-art scene.

www.treluce.com

Gerold Tusch

(*1969) studied painting and ceramics at the Universität Mozarteum in Salzburg, Austria, the Gerrit Rietveld Akademie in Amsterdam, and the 4th Biennial European Academies of Visual Arts, Maastricht, the Netherlands. Working mostly in ceramics, his works range from small objects to installations, which he has exhibited in numerous solo and group exhibitions.

gerold.tusch@aon.at

Vitra

was founded in 1950 and made a name for itself as a manufacturer of progressive, modern furniture by names such as Charles & Ray Eames and George Nelson. It has continued this tradition and developed a wide range of furnishings for the office, the home and public spaces in collaboration with a long list of top designers, including Ronan & Erwan Bouroullec, Hella Jongerius, Ron Arad, Arik Levy, Jasper Morrison, Isamu Noguchi, Verner Panton and Philippe Starck. Vitra's chairman is Rolf Fehlbaum, son of the company's founder.

www.vitra.com

WIS Design

are Lisa Widén and Anna Irinarchos. Both graduated from Beckmans College of Design in Stockholm in 2006. With a poetic and playful approach, WIS offers fresh contemporary design in several media: furniture, product, interior and graphics.

www.wisdesign.se

Philip Michael Wolfson / Wolfson Design

(*1958) studied at the Cornell University School of Architecture in Ithaca, USA and the Architectural Association in London. After graduating he worked with Zaha Hadid at the outset of her career. In 1991 he set up his own design practice, Wolfson Design, and has worked predominantly on residential interiors and exhibition pieces for Contrasts Gallery, Phillips de Pury & Company, The Apartment, R 20th Century Design and Design Miami/Basel. His designs are greatly inspired by the early experiments of the Russian and Italian Modernist movements.

www.wolfsondesign.com

Richard Wright / Wright

founded the Chicago-based auction house Wright in 2000. Specialising in modern and contemporary design, it has become one of the key auction houses in this field. The sales feature historic and cutting-edge design alongside post-war and contemporary art, and encourage the recent synergy of the art and design industries. Wright has been also credited with raising the industry bar for catalogue quality, with specially commissioned photography and dynamic, original layouts.

www.wright20.com

Tokujin Yoshioka

(*1967) graduated from Kuwasawa Design School and continued to study design with Shiro Kuramata and Issey Miyake. In 2000 he set up his own studio, working for clients such as Swarovski, Issey Miyake, Hermès, Moroso, Lexus, Peugeot and BMW. His works are part of the permanent collections at the Vitra Design Museum, Weil am Rhein, MoMA, New York, Centre Pompidou, Paris, Victoria & Albert Museum, London, the Pinakothek der Moderne, Munich, and many others.

www.tokujin.com

James Zemaitis

is director of the twentieth century design department at Sotheby's New York. Zemaitis' auction career began in 1996 at Christie's. He later went on to become worldwide head of 20th- and 21st-century design at Phillips de Pury & Company before joining Sotheby's in 2003. He is co-author, together with Alexander Payne, of The Coffee Table Coffee Table Book (2003, Black Dog/Phaidon).

Concept and texts: Sophie Lovell
Picture editor: Asia Kornacki
Additional research: Asia Kornacki and Ali Winstanley
www.sophielovell.com

Project management and editing: Ulrike Ruh and Berit Liedtke

Copy editing: Marcy Goldberg, Susan James and Markus Zehentbauer

Art Direction, design and layout: Ringen
Cover image design and concept: Ringen
Cover 3D rendering: Rune Spaans
Cover background image: Thorsten Klapsch
Limited Edition font: Ringen

Special thanks to: Steve and Rilla Alexander, Helge Aszmoneit, Marcus
Gaab, Barbara Glasner, Jasper Hagenberg, Thorsten Klapsch, Orlando
Lovell, Micke Lund, Angelika Taschen, Rolf Teloh, Gerrit Terstiege and
all the contributors, their assistants and their agents who gave so
much of their time, patience, images and thoughts to help make this
book possible.

Library of Congress Control Number: 2008941511

Bibliographic information published by the German National Library
The German National Library lists this publication in the Deutsche
Nationalbibliografie; detailed bibliographic data are available on the
Internet at http://dnb.d-nb.de.

This book is also available in a German language edition
(ISBN 978-3-7643-8894-2).

© 2009 Birkhäuser Verlag AG
Basel · Boston · Berlin
P.O. Box 133, CH-4010 Basel, Switzerland
Part of Springer Science+Business Media

Printed on acid-free paper produced from chlorine-free pulp. TCF ∞

Printed in Germany

ISBN 978-3-7643-8895-9

9 8 7 6 5 4 3 2 1
www.birkhauser.ch